"God's Word for Warriors" is a succinct and comprehensive resource for a reintegrating veteran I would have loved to read as I was navigating life returning home. As a medic having served with combat arms while deployed, I felt a sense of hypocrisy and difficulty articulating how to defend my position as a maturing Christian. This text summarizes in analytical fashion how a veteran may wield a weapon and simultaneously preserve life at war, and return home with honor morally and spiritually.

Sergeant Jacob L. Schultz
Army National Guard, Operation Enduring Freedom.
Former student at Lipscomb University and
now a student in medical school.

"I started my transition as a veteran in the God's Word for Warrior course with Dr. Seals. Dr. Seals created a safe environment where we discussed tough topics that only veterans would understand. As a female it was intimidating entering the classroom with the majority of students were males. However, it was easy to look past that once we got to know each other. I am not the type to talk too much in front of strangers, but the openness of the classroom made it very easy to do so. The course book was an excellent resource that created discussions in the course. The God's Word for Warrior course opened my eyes to issues I was struggling with in my life. I cannot thank Dr. Seals enough for his patience, kindness and compassion. I will never forget him or the lessons I learned in God's Word for Warrior course."

~ ~ ~ ~ ~ ~ Theresa Benner
Freedom.
Pres   niversity).

D1403242

"Returning from combat is hard; transitioning back into a civilian role is harder. Dr. Seals eloquently tackles the very real issues today's veterans face after service. "God's word for the warriors" challenges Veterans to face the issues from their service instead of trying to forget them. This book isn't a Doctor trying to tell people an easier way to transition but rather a fellow veteran using scripture to guide veterans through transitioning. One of the most helpful books I have read and recommend to any service member transitioning back to society."

Bryan S. Flanery
Sergeant U.S. Army retired, National Outreach
Coordinator Reboot Combat Recovery.
Presently student at Lipscomb University.

"U.S. Marine, Biblical Scholar, Christian Minister. Dr. Seals brings all of his experience, knowledge and passion to produce this nuanced yet practical guide to post 9/11 veterans returning home. This book is to those who have faithfully followed orders to follow Christ who is faithful to provide the healing, direction, and hope they need during their difficult time of transition."

-Steve Parham M.Div, MSCMHC,
M.Ed, Christian Counselor

"Tom Seals has dedicated much of his distinguished career to helping veterans make the transition from combat leader to family, church, and community leader. Tom possesses a remarkable gift of partnering with veteran students in and out of the classroom in authentic relationship designed to help students discern God's calling for their life and how God can use anyone's past as the foundation for work in the Kingdom. "God's Word for Warriors" is the culmination of years of Tom's work counseling, leading, and empowering veterans to define themselves the way God defines them - as children of the King."

Joshua M. Roberts
Dean of Student Development, Lipscomb University

"I was in Tom's first course using this book's text, a course geared toward veterans and it truly was a transformative experience in my life. The class started in a traditional setting, but with Tom's insight developed into more of a group counseling session. We bonded in that class through our shared experience as veterans. I have completed my Bachelor of Science degree in Psychology and am currently attending dental school and this is still the most important class I have taken, and Tom is the only former instructor that I still have a relationship with.

Derelmy "Randell" Buckley
Former CWO, U.S. Army

God's Word *for* WARRIORS

RETURNING HOME FOLLOWING DEPLOYMENT

THOMAS L. SEALS

WESTBOW
PRESS®
A DIVISION OF THOMAS NELSON
& ZONDERVAN

WestBow Press books may be ordered through booksellers or by contacting:

WestBow Press
A Division of Thomas Nelson & Zondervan
1663 Liberty Drive
Bloomington, IN 47403
www.westbowpress.com
1 (866) 928-1240

ISBN: 978-1-5127-3263-4 (sc)
ISBN: 978-1-5127-3264-1 (hc)
ISBN: 978-1-5127-3319-8 (e)

Library of Congress Control Number: 2016903252

Print information available on the last page.

WestBow Press rev. date: 03/10/2016

To Barbara, my wife, companion, and fellow worker
in God's kingdom and the many men and women who served so
faithfully and honorably in service to their nation and its citizens.

Contents

Preface

Having served in the US Marine Corps, the US Government in Europe, and now in the capacity of teaching in the College of Bible and Ministry at Lipscomb University in Nashville, Tennessee, I have had many opportunities to work and serve side by side and fellowship with some of the finest men and women in America, our servicemen and women. I count it a privilege to have been blessed with this opportunity.

At the present time, I have the added privilege of teaching many of these former and present military personnel in a university setting. It is my daily prayer that the Lord God may use my past experiences and education to assist these individuals in their continuing education and preparation to serve their communities following deployment.

This publication is an attempt to assist these veterans in their return to civilian life and to successfully navigate through the challenges many of them face in acclimating to a culture and society that is different in many ways from their experiences in the military, especially in combat zones. If God can use me and my attempts to offer some beneficial insights and experiences that may help these veterans, I will consider my efforts worthwhile.

Introduction

As an American veteran, you return home from deployment(s) and combat zones, and you have witnessed experiences that millions of your fellow countrymen and women have never experienced. The fact is that the vast majority of Americans do not have a clue as to what you have experienced. In addition, veterans are returning to their homeland and filtering back into a society that, in many ways, is so foreign to what they have experienced in the past several months, even years in their deployment(s). What you desire is to establish some stability, peace, and strength in your life once again. One of the major problems that many of you in this situation confront is the fact that it is often difficult to "connect with supportive people and new opportunities."[1]

With this book, we begin a new journey as we consider the various subjects of the chapters set forth in this work. To the veteran who is reading this introduction, we are asking you to take this first step, a step that Jesus asked of four men in Mark 1:14–21, which says, "Follow me." Nothing religious happened in this encounter with Jesus—no prayer, no confession of faith, no religious questions asked by Jesus. These four men didn't know much about Jesus and probably just a little about God. Yet they followed Jesus, and now we know how the story of these four apostles of Christ ended.

---

[1] David Dobbs, "A New Focus on the 'Post' in Post-Traumatic Stress," *The New York Times*, December 25, 2012, D2.

This may be such a moment for us. We are being called to engage in a new walk, a walk that will carry us back into a culture we have been away from for months and maybe years. These four apostles in Mark were standing right in the midst of life, fishing and working at their vocations. Were they thinking about God? Probably not, but God was thinking of them. So Jesus said to them (and to us), "Follow me."

Our Lord did not speak religious words. He just asked something of these disciples. It must have looked simple on the surface, but it was not. Nor was it particularly enticing. Yet when they followed, they came to know that there was much more to life than simply fishing and taking some fish home for the family. Life is more than jobs, a bowling night, a Super Bowl, or a vacation. Mark opened this scenario with these words: "Jesus came into Galilee, preaching the gospel of God, and saying, 'The time is fulfilled, and the kingdom of God is at hand; repent, and believe in the gospel'" (Mark 1:14–15). I think that Mark would say to us that what happened to these four men is what Jesus invites us to as well. God is at hand. He is very near to us. He is always present, always opening doors, always challenging us.

I cannot predict the results of committing to this new venture, this "returning home following deployment." I cannot tell you what it will mean for you individually. It may open a completely new way of life for you, a journey down a new road. But I can assure you of one thing, God will be with you, and you will never be alone.

This journey through *God's Word for Warriors* resolves to address several situations that you as an American soldier face in your goal toward normalcy in your post-deployment future. To assist you in *reconnecting* with your culture, this book begins with the principle that the first reconnection must contain a spiritual or faith component. Through the topics of this book, we hope to address many of the various post-deployment issues. Hopefully, we will establish a growing and deepening relationship with God and fellow believers. Through this course of study, we will strive to bring to each of us a wholeness of life—spiritually, socially, and physically—a life that our Lord desires for all: "I came that they may have life, and have it abundantly" (John 10:10).

Chapter 1

The Bible, the Ante-Nicene Fathers, and Warfare

One of the first challenges faced by a returning veteran may be an encounter with those who may be antagonistic toward any war effort ... or even toward the warriors themselves. Therefore, it is imperative that a believer-warrior be aware of what the Bible and history have said about whether or not a person of faith can serve in a war effort. Consequently, our first inquiry will be to determine what the Scriptures and early Christian fathers had to say about this matter.

The Bible records many wars throughout its pages, both in the Old and New Testaments. When the Lord God created humanity and all of creation, he pronounced that everything and every situation was good (Genesis 1:31). In this good creation, God created *Adam*, and he gave to *Adam* a free will, thus giving him the right to choose between good and evil. Because humans chose to violate God's goodness, we now live in an environment where evil and good are at war with each other.

With God's boundaries violated by humans, the Lord established ruling authorities that would make and enforce the laws he provided. This started early in the years following creation with the advent of the Noachian and Abrahamic covenants. However, with the birth of Israel as a "called out" community of God's people, the laws that set boundaries for the people became a system of laws governing the nation. This system, also known as a covenant, compact, or agreement, governed the nation in relation to God, neighbors, and the self. God knew that an unregenerate society without such restraints would seek to destroy all that was good, and that's the reason we need this covenant. And this covenant included the establishment of civil military-type forces to keep order, protect people from threatening invaders, and maintain law and order within the borders of God's own people.

What does the Bible say about such forces? In the Hebrew Scriptures (the Old Testament), there are, in fact, certain guidelines about such forces.

1. Age and qualifications: God directed his people to take a census of the tribes of Israel and to draft young men to make up this army of enforcers. These young men were at least twenty years of age and physically fit (Numbers 1:2–4; Deuteronomy 20:8).
2. Training and pay: All the tribes of Israel were open and could be called into active service to maintain God's righteous cause for the nation (Deuteronomy 20:9; 2 Chronicles 25:5–6).
3. Priests: As today's chaplains, priests were not used for combat but were called upon to spiritually serve the military (Numbers 1:47; Deuteronomy 20:1–4).
4. Gender and age: Women and children were excluded from service. Deborah was used in a leadership capacity as judge, not in combat (Judges 4).
5. Exemptions: The Hebrew Scriptures listed several reasons that could excuse men from serving, including those who had purchased new land (Deuteronomy 20:5), those who had just planted vineyards (Deuteronomy 20:6), those who had just recently become engaged (Deuteronomy 20:7), and those who had just gotten married (Deuteronomy 24:5).

6. Battlefield instructions: These included the treatment of prisoners, women, and children, and it even included moral codes governing how to treat the conquered land and laws for personal hygiene (Deuteronomy 20:19; 23:12–13).
7. Rules of engagement: The Israelites were first commanded to seek peace with the enemy if possible. If the enemy refused such offers, then the army could attack (Deuteronomy 20:10–12; 1 Kings 20:31ff). This situation in war is clearly depicted in the narrative concerning Ben-Hadad, king of Aram.
8. Representative: The Israelites also had to remember to act in battle as directed by the Lord God—that is, they were to serve as his appointed representatives, not murderers (Deuteronomy 7).

The Old Testament and Warriors

We ask now, "What does the Old Testament have to say about warriors?" A casual reading reveals examples of Old Testament warriors. Note the following examples:

- Abraham was one of the earliest leaders of an army (Genesis 14:14–15).
- Moses and Joshua were chosen to lead Israel into many battles.
- Judges 5:23 actually curses a town for not engaging in war in support of Israel.
- Saul was the first king of Israel and formed a permanent army (1 Samuel 13:2; 24:2; 26:2).
- The psalmist states that David was trained by God for battle (Psalm 18:34).
- David increased the army, hiring troops from other nations (2 Samuel 15:19–22).
- Later David established a military system of rotating troops (1 Chronicles 27).

- Although his reign was peaceful, Solomon added horsemen and chariots (1 Kings 10:26).
- God himself ordered Israel into battle and commanded his own army (2 Kings 6:15–19).
- Proverbs 24:6 speaks of the fact that one can "wage your war" but only with "counselors."
- In Israel, there was a developing contingent of temple "soldiers" or "police" who served at the beck and call of the chief priests.
- In listing "heroes of the faith" in the Old Testament, the writer of Hebrews stated that he didn't have enough time to list the heroes who "conquered kingdoms … became mighty in war, put foreign armies to flight" (Hebrews 11:33–35).

The New Testament and Warriors

As previously outlined, the Old Testament has many examples of figures depicting, preparing for, and engaging in war, but what about the New Testament? Does the New Testament speak of warriors? We have many passages in the New Testament that refer to military situations through the use of analogies (e.g., Jesus in Luke 14:31–32). There are, in fact, several verses that may be directly related to military situations.

- John the Baptizer encountered soldiers, yet he never asked them to resign (Luke 3:14).
- In Matthew 8:5–13, Jesus commends a centurion's faith, yet he does not advise him to abandon his career.
- At the cross another centurion acknowledges Jesus as a god or Son of God (Matthew 27:54).
- In Acts 10, Peter is introduced to a God-fearing centurion named Cornelius, who, to our knowledge, was never advised to leave the army.
- Paul refers to believers in the household of Caesar, which could include soldiers (Philippians 4:2).

- Paul spent years with various centurions in his travels and imprisonments, but he apparently never encouraged them to leave the military. In fact, Paul sets forth a general principle that may be applied to soldiers as well when he was speaking of marriage, "Everyone should remain in the state in which he was called" (1 Corinthians 7:20).

What we have seen thus far in this brief survey is that both Old and New Testaments reveal the fact that armies have been created to maintain justice and security in the nation. In addition, God has set forth biblical principles to guide the Christian in his or her relationship with such governments and their authority (cf. Romans 13:1–7; 1 Peter 2:13–14). Military and police forces are often necessary to ensure the security of a people. For those who believe the establishment of military forces is the thing that creates situations where war becomes a reality must confront the possibility that, as the saying goes, "The military exists because of war. War does not exist because of the military." We must recognize also that the God of the Old Testament is also the God of the New Testament. If military force is sometimes necessary in the former days and is authorized by God, is this truth not also applicable in the present era? After all, God does not change (Malachi 3:6; James 1:19).

The Ante-Nicene Fathers and Warriors

This period of history begins with the apostolic age and concludes with the First Council of Nicaea in 325 CE.[2] The purpose of a survey of this period of history is to discover what the fathers of this age had to say about the military and the Christian. The Nicene Creed was a confession of faith adopted in 325 CE and accepted as the orthodox beliefs of the early church.

---

[2] This particular creed was the church's first ecumenical council called by Emperor Constantine to deal with Arianism. Its creed affirmed the divinity of Jesus as of the same substance (Gk. *homoousios*) with God the Father.

From that, we understand that many faithful men in the Bible have been members of the military, and nowhere in biblical recorded history has the military service of believers been questioned from the standpoint of rightness or wrongness. It was assumed that individuals would serve in this capacity when the need arose. So we ask now, "What do the Ante-Nicene Fathers have to say about warriors and military responsibilities to the nation?" We recognize, of course, that most of the Christians in the early years of the church were Jewish, and the church was initially seen as a Jewish sect. Thus, they were typically exempted from service in the Roman Army.

From our brief survey here, apparently the early church made no laws that forbid Christians from serving in the military forces of their day. Neither the Old Testament nor Jesus and the New Testament, as far as our records reveal, strictly forbid believers from serving as warriors.

In the early centuries of the church, history confirms that persecution against the church became a reality. Believers were arrested, imprisoned, and even executed. In these hostile times and environments, several of the early church fathers discouraged military service, but others supported it.

- Polycarp (70–155 CE), bishop of Smyrna and one of the earliest writers, did not utter one word against war or Christians engaged in the military.
- Clement of Alexander (153–217 CE), famous theologian from Egypt, wrote, "Practice husbandry, we say, if you are a husbandman; but while you till the fields, know God. Sail the sea, you who are devoted to navigation, yet call the whilst on the heavenly pilot. Has (saving) knowledge taken hold of you while engaged in military service? Listen to the commander who orders what is right."[3]

---

[3] Wilson, William, trans., *Ante-Nicene Fathers*, Vol. 2. New York: Christian Literature Publishing., Co. 1885.

- Tertullian (160–220 CE), one of the best known as evident in his treatise, *The Crown*, speaks of a Christian soldier who refused to wear the appropriate headdress laurel and was subsequently mocked, stripped of his commission, and imprisoned to await death. However, this narrative reveals that believers were, in fact, serving in the military. He opposed Christians participating in the army because of the moral and spiritual evils associated with such. However, he wrote, "Without ceasing, for all our emperors we offer prayer. We pray for life prolonged; for security to the empire; for protection to the imperial house; for brave armies."

- The Roman emperor Marcus Aurelius (121–180 CE) gives us clear evidence of Christian presence in the military. As reported by S. J. Edward A. Ryan,[4] with a sharp decline in population coupled with the growing threat of barbarian hordes, there was a massive conscription into the military, giving Christians the choice between serving (or paying a sum for a substitute) or refusal at the cost of their lives. This made it inevitable that Christians would be found among the Legionnaires. It was this situation that no doubt moved Tertullian to write extensively about the moral arguments against Christians serving. In fact, his *Apologeticum* criticized believers for their presence in the palace, the senate, the forum, and the army.

- Hippolytus (170–236 CE) opposed Christians being involved in military service and listed military service as an occupation to be avoided by church membership. He listed it with other professions like pimping, sculpting idols, prostitution, and being a magician, all professions associated with immorality or idolatry.

- Eusebius, bishop in Caesarea (263–339 CE), informs us that Christians were serving in governmental positions

---

[4] S. J. Edward Ryan, "The Rejection of Military Service by the Early Christians," *Theological Studies* (February 1952), 13:1–32.

and in the army long before Diocletian (244–311 CE) was Caesar.[5] Eusebius further informs us that some believers were allowed to refrain from offering sacrifices to the Roman gods.[6] However, later Diocletian ordered commanders to dismiss Christians from service if they refused to offer sacrifices.

- Lactantius (240–320 CE), an early Christian writer and advisor to the first Christian Roman emperor, Constantine I, served under Diocletian before his conversion to Christianity. Diocletian was noted for his persecution of Christians. Lactantius reports that Christian attendants to Diocletian made the sign of the cross when fortune-tellers were trying to divine the future for the emperor. For this act, Diocletian sent out letters commanding all Christians to be dishonorably discharged from the military.[7]

What we see from this survey is many early church fathers did not address the military question. For example, we possess no writings from Mathetes (130 CE), Polycarp (155 CE), Ignatius (30–107 CE), Papias (70–155 CE), Justin Martyr (110–165 CE), the epistle of Barnabas (100 CE), Ireneas (120–202 CE), the Shepherd of Hermes (160 CE), Tatian (110–172 CE), or Athenagoras (177 CE) concerning whether Christians can or cannot serve in war or even if war is justified.

The previously listed fathers, however, reveal to us that Christians were indeed serving in the Roman government and army, and although some individuals, such as Tertullian, were against military service, the early churches did not have a consensus view,

---

[5] McGiffert, Arthur Cushman, trans. *Nicene and Post-Nicene Fathers, Second Series*, Vol. 1. Buffalo, NY: Christian Literature Publishing Co. 1890.

[6] Ibid.

[7] Tower, James, comment on John Helgeland, "Christians in the Roman Army, AD 173-337," "The Tower Blog, December 27, 2012, http://practicingresurrection together.wordpress.com/2012/12/27/pacifism-and-military-service-in-the early-church-a-short-history.html.

Evidently, early Christianity had a diversity of opinion and practice on this issue of military service. Then, too, we have archaeological evidence of Christian tombstones that identify individuals with their rank and name of their legion.[8]

---

[8] For further information on war and the Christian, see Appendix: The Christian and War.

Chapter 2

The Just War Theory

The church from the beginning has struggled with the question of warfare. Many believe that the teachings of Jesus prohibited the use of the sword. There may have been a strong pacifist standing among some of the early Christians for the first three hundred years, but this started to change after Constantine became emperor and made Christianity the official Roman religion. The early church fathers debated this issue for centuries, and out of such debates came the "just war theory," a theory that dates back to the holy wars of the Old Testament. The theory was developed by Augustine (354–430 CE) and was refined by Thomas Aquinas (1224–74), and it basically listed six conditions for a just war.

1. It must be conducted by a legitimate authority that explicitly serves notice stating that it intends to use military power to attain its objectives.
2. The cause must be just—that is, the action must be intended for the advancement of good or for the avoidance of evil, defensive and not aggressive.
3. It must be undertaken only as a last resort.
4. The good anticipated from the war must outweigh the evil done in pursuit of the war, without any accompanying hatred, animosity, and thirst for revenge.

5. There must be a reasonable expectation of success in the effort. This is like the king in Jesus' parable who "counted the cost" (Luke 14:31–32) before going to war. The success is the achievement of the *just* cause for which the war was begun.

6. If war became a reality, it must be conducted according to the internationally accepted rules of warfare, never going beyond certain agreed-upon moral constraints. This prohibits attacks on nonmilitary targets, including civilians, unnecessary destruction, looting, and massacres.

In our modern society there are basically three distinct positions regarding the participation of Christians in war.[9]

First, many view such participation as a responsibility of Christian citizenship, drawing their conclusions from Paul's word in Romans 13:1, which says, "Let every person be subject to the governing authorities. For there is no authority except from God, and those that exist have been instituted by God." It is important to note that Paul states that any state official is "God's servant" to reward the good citizen and punish the evildoer. Does this include Hitler, Stalin, or Saddam? In addition, three times Paul repeats that the state's "authority" is God's authority and that the state's "ministry" is God's ministry (vv. 4a, 4b, 6).

This is a strong affirmation that God has established the state with authority and that when it is punishing injustice and evil, it is doing God's will. Resistance to the state is justified only if the state claimed ultimate authority and thus assumed the place of God. When the nation is involved in a just war, it is done to protect the people against a foreign threatening power and to safeguard the well-being of citizens.

Of course, in the United States, citizens have the right to be conscientious objectors. However, I feel that they need to serve their

---

[9] Roger H. Crook, *An Introduction to Christian Ethics* (Upper Saddle River, NJ: Prentice Hall, 1999), pp. 223-224.

Thomas L. Seals

country in some manner (Peace Corps, Corpsmen, etc.) and that they also need to pray for the welfare of their country.

In the last resort, we know that the use of force in world affairs is necessary because of oppressive and tyrannical powers at work. If someone does not step up to try to prevent such powers from developing, evil tyrants may extend their control until they dominate the rest of the world.

Second, some believe that their commitment to Christ prohibits any involvement in armed conflict, resorting to pacifism as the answer. Most of these do not see this refusal to participate as a strategy but as a way God intends believers to live. These individuals are pacifists not in order to achieve peace but in grateful personal obedience to the God of love. They are aware of the evil in the world and realistic about aggression and oppression, but they work to overcome those in peaceful ways. Pacifists of this bent believe that discipleship calls for love rather than hate and that war can never be an expression of love.

Third, some Christians believe that war is sometimes the lesser of two evils and that worse evil may result from a failure to resist aggression and oppression. The term often applied to this position is "agonized participation," and with this methodology, people give conditional support to the government. These individuals evaluate the situation for themselves and support the government only in those situations they believe necessary.

This "agonized participation" theory is very close to the just war theory, and it is outlined by Edward LeRoy Long in his book, *War and Conscience in America.*

a) This position believes that while war can never be an act of justice, it may sometimes be necessary for the prevention of a greater evil that would result from permitting morally perverse power to gain political dominance.

b) The agonized participant insists that war must be conducted with contrition and kept free of vindictive hatred for the enemy.

c) Military victory, while necessary, is but a negative attainment that clears the way for subsequent political and social programs designed to reestablish reasonable justice and order (p. 45).

d) Lastly, the agonized participant acknowledges the right and privilege of conscientious objection to war, even though he disagrees with those Christians who consider themselves called to this witness.[10]

In view of these things, we still ask the question, "How can we resolve the apparent discrepancy between God's call to love our enemies and the call for punishment of evildoers as set forth in Romans 12:17–21 and Romans 13:1–7?" But notice also that the contrast between forgiveness and punishment is not only *between* these paragraphs but embodied *within* the first.

The first prohibition, "Repay no one evil for evil," is followed by the prohibition, "Beloved, never avenge yourselves," which is follow by, "Vengeance is mine, I will repay, says the Lord." So the reason why wrath, revenge, and retribution are forbidden is not because they are in themselves wrong reactions to evil but because they are God's prerogative. Thus, when state authorities are called upon to wage a just war, they are being used as God's instruments or ministers.

Every Christian is called upon to be a peacemaker. The Beatitudes are given as descriptions of how individual Christians are supposed to shape their characters. We may never establish utopia on earth. Christ's kingdom of righteousness and peace may never become universal. Yet we must always strive to become what Christ calls us to become, for "blessed are the peacemakers."

---

[10] Edward LeRoy Long, *War and Conscience in America* (Philadelphia: Westminster Press, 1968), 41, 44, 46.

Chapter 3

The Importance of a Faith Community

Two are better than one, because they have a good
return for their toil. For if they fall, one will lift up
his fellow; but woe to him who is alone when he falls
and has not another to lift him up ... And though a
man might prevail against one who is alone, two will
withstand him. A threefold cord is not quickly broken.

—Ecclesiastes 4:9–10, 12

We live in a very individualistic world.[11] However, we truly do need
one another. "It is not good that the man should be alone" (Genesis
2:18). Those were the very words of our Creator, God. In addition,
those around us need the same thing from us—companionship or
community. We need to share our lives, struggles, prayers, hopes,
and joys with one another. We must be ready, in the words of the
writer of Hebrews, "to stir up one another to love and good works"
(Hebrews 10:24).

---

[11] Israel's salvation was corporate, whereas in our religious culture salvation
is erroneously viewed as individualistic!

As veterans, we need a safe haven, a place where we can go to relax, regroup, and receive good news and encouragement. Then we will be ready to go back into the world again. This common need of humanity is one of the reasons and purposes of the faith community that God created.

Yet the fact is that many of us have decided that we would be better served if we did not become involved with a faith community. We, therefore, tend to self-isolate, avoiding crowds, people, and the church. However, this avoidance lifestyle is certainly a creation of man, not God. So too, we rob the society around us of an opportunity to fully benefit from our experiences and talents.

Simon and Garfunkel, writing during the Vietnam War, described the isolation troops' self-talk,

> Hiding in my room, safe within my womb,
> I touch no one and no one touches me.
> I am a rock, I am an island.
> And a rock feels no pain; and an island never cries.
> (*Sounds of Silence*)

In the military we leave behind our old group of friends and develop new ones. In the military environment, we get to know one another in unique ways. We are comfortable with one another's likes and dislikes, how we react in certain situations, what makes another person mad or joyful. We have similar priorities and goals, and we are okay with one another's hang-ups. We respect and depend on one another.

But then we come home and things are different. We can't seem to reconnect with our old friends. They have moved on in life, leaving us behind. Crowds make us anxious. Loud noises send us diving for cover. We fear new places and new stresses. In fact, we seem strange in comparison to others. We appear to ourselves as outsiders. No one seems to like us, and we begin to think something is wrong with us. So we become isolated as we run away. Social isolation seems like the best option, and it feels comfortable—at least at first! It seems easier than dealing with people we don't understand. In reality, however, this is the worse move we can make.

Again, we must remember that isolation goes against the very basic design of our Creator God. He made us to be a communal species. The faith community is designed specifically to address and avoid these kinds of feelings of isolation.

I want us to consider for a moment a passage in the book of Joshua. The passage says, "And the seven priests bearing the seven trumpets of rams' horns before the ark of the Lord passed on ... So the people shouted, and the trumpets were blown. As soon as the people heard the sound of the trumpet, the people raised a great shout, and the wall fell down flat" (Joshua 6:13, 20). The walls came tumbling down!

Is it not time for us to bring down the *invisible* walls (although we mentally perceive these walls clearly) that are leading us to avoid a faith community of some kind? We may ask, "Does God care? Do the faith communities care?" But these aren't the real questions. We must ask, "Do we care?"

I believe we can find glasses that will help clear our vision and enable us to see that God and faith communities really care. Attitudes can be changed, and perceptions cleared up. But to win the battle, we must do more than just talk. We must march, blow our trumpets, and tear down the invisible walls! And as Jesus states in Luke, "Why do you see the speck that is in your brother's eye, but do not notice the log in your own eye?" (Luke 6:41).

When we divorce ourselves from the faith community, we rob ourselves of a great opportunity for spiritual support. I believe it is within faith communities that we are presented with the best opportunity to grow and develop spiritually, physically, and emotionally. Furthermore, while we might be prone to look at our own inadequacies, we must not fail to look at our internal attributes or overlook the power we can exercise by being there for others who may be sitting in silence and feeling alone.

Participation in faith communities can enable us to realize that we are people who can help others instead of people who need help.

Such a realization is a major factor in rebuilding our self-esteem and confidence.

The word *religion* is derived from the Latin word *reflixio. Lixio* is translated as *ligament* or *connection.* Therefore, religion is the means of reconnection with God. It is the result of the conviction that God loves us and desires us to be a part of his faith community, which is where we embrace the grand possibility of gaining spiritual strength.

Scripture repeatedly informs us that God desires us to come to him. He wants us in his presence, and he wants us to have a place of refuge and peace, a sanctuary from the world. He desires that we hear his voice of love and compassion, and we are also afforded the opportunity to let him hear from us.

Who are we? Obviously we are all special. All are created in the image of God. First and foremost, however, we are individuals who possess a spiritual base through which God has offered to enter our lives with love and strength. We are individuals who have the ability to perceive not only our own needs but also the needs of others. And we are enabled by God to respond to these needs in a helpful manner.

A recent survey of veterans by the Pew Research Center entitled, "The Military-Civilian Gap: War and Sacrifice in the Post-9/11 Era," reported that 27 percent of veterans reported that readjustment to civilian life was either "somewhat difficult" or "very difficult." In addition, this research reported that 67 percent of these veterans identified attending a faith community at least weekly as the most important variable associated with an easy and successful reentry into civilian life. The Pew Center reported also that faith communities were second only to the military itself as "institutions" in which veterans have a "great deal" or "quite a lot" of confidence.[12]

---

[12] Rudd, David. Written Statement of M. David Rudd, PhD, ABPP before the U.S. House of Representatives Committee on Veterans' Affairs Subcommittee of Health on Building Bridges between VA and Community Organizations to Support Veterans and Families, February 27, 2012. Pew Research Center http://www.apa.org/about/gr/issues/military/david-rudd.aspx.

In a 2007 Gallup poll, 86 percent of respondents indicated a belief in God, while only 6 percent stated they did not believe in God. Many of these individuals, as the previous Pew Research Center stated, would describe religion or spirituality as the most important source of their strength and direction in life. Research also indicates that healthy religious practices or spirituality is often associated with lower levels of symptoms and clinical problems such as PTSD or depression. For example, anger, rage, and a desire for revenge following trauma may be tempered by forgiveness, spiritual beliefs, or spiritual practices.[13] Thus, recovery of meaningful life, or "abundant life," as set forth by Jesus in John 10:10, may be achieved through changed ways of thinking, involvement in meaningful faith communities, and ritual experienced as part of religious or spiritual exercises.

Researchers noted that after the 9/11 terrorist attacks, 90 percent of respondents reported turning to "prayer, religion or spiritual feelings, as a coping mechanism."[14] In general, research suggests there is a positive association between spirituality and grief recovery for survivors of traumatic loss. For many, spiritual exercises provide a frame through which recovery occurs.[15] Additionally, there are great benefits from supportive relationships often provided by faith communities.[16]

We must recognize that the faith community we are talking about here is not a church building. It is a living organism composed

---

[13] R. W. Hood, P. C. Hill, and B. Spika, *The Psychology of Religion: An Empirical Approach* (2009), 179.

[14] Schuster, Mark A., Stein, Bradley D., Jaycox, Lisa H., Collins, Rebecca L., Marshall, Grant N., Elliott, Marc N., Zhou, Annie J., Kanouse, David E., Morrison, Janina L., and Berry, Sandra H. *New England Journal of Medicine*, 345 (20): 1507–12.

[15] Jennifer H. Wortman and Crystal L. Park, "Religion and Spirituality in Adjustment Following Bereavement: An Integrative Review," in *Death Studies*, ed. Robert A. Neimeyer (Taylor & Francis Group, 2015), 703-736.

[16] DN McIntosh and RC Silver "Religion's Role in Adjustment to a Negative Life Event: Coping with the Loss of a Child,"*Journal of Personality and Social Psychology* 65 (1993): 812–21.

of like-minded believers. The Scriptures refer to this community as "the body of Christ." Christ is the head, and believers are the hands and feet. The apostle Paul gives us this corporate image in his letter to believers at Corinth (1 Corinthians 12:4-11).

The following are passages from Scripture that relate to the topic at hand. You, the reader, may wish to reflect on each passage in relation to the following questions: What is the main point, and how does it apply to my personal situation as a returning veteran? Consider 1 Corinthians 12:14–26, Proverbs 27:17, Romans 12:15–16, Romans 15:1–2, Hebrews 3:13, and 1 John 3:18.

> In speaking on the importance of community
> and the strength received from being together,
> Chris Adsit writes the following story designed to
> encourage veterans experiencing combat trauma:
> What Happens Underground?

Have you ever spent time in Northern California and walked among the majestic redwood trees in the various parks there? These are the tallest and most massive trees on the planet, many of them ascending more than 350 feet. Some are four thousand years old. You can't help but become awestruck by their strength, endurance, and tenacity.

But think for a minute. Have you ever seen a redwood tree growing all by itself in the middle of a field? Probably not. Well, not unless the area around it was recently cleared by man. And if so, it won't stand there for long. God has ordained that redwood trees must always live in groves, because He is aware of their secret— *shallow root systems.*

Unlike many trees that have deep taproots, redwood root systems grow laterally, and cover a huge area to efficiently absorb the small amount rain that falls on their often rocky habitat. So in order to keep from being blown over, redwoods *interlace* their roots below the surface, forming a solid platform that stretches for acres, even miles. When the storms blow through their valleys, they remain standing because they hold one another up!

This is an excellent picture of how the Christian community is supposed to work. The world can be a stormy place from time to time. As a combat veteran, you've been in some of the worse storms in history. Any Christian—even someone who isn't a veteran—who tries to go it alone is vulnerable. It won't be long before these people encounter difficulties that are more than they were designed to handle by themselves. This is why it is necessary for Christians to get involved in one another's lives, interlace their *roots*, and hold one another up during the storms that come along.[17]

---

[17] Chris Adsit, "What Happens Underground?" *The Combat Trauma Healing Manual* (Newport News, VA: Military Ministry Press, 2007), 50.

Chapter 4

Relationships: God, Family, and Friends

The warrior returning home from deployment faces numerous challenges, challenges that will vary from individual to individual. The leading challenges are present in the area of fellowship—relationships with God, family, and friends. Part of the adjustment in rejoining civilian life and establishing relationships is figuring how to communicate one's experience with war. This can be especially challenging for veterans with post-traumatic stress disorder (PTSD).

In his book *On Combat*, Lt. Col. Dave Grossman, chaplain at the Charles Wright Academy, writes that healing is found in "the power of telling our stories honestly in a trusted circle of compatriots. What a remarkably unmiraculous salvation, yet profound as grace: men can be healed through telling their stories in community!"[18] Veterans desire to find somebody who is there for them and supports them. That is crucial.

The US Department of Veteran Affairs reports that many survivors with PTSD have problems with trust, closeness, communication, and problem solving.[19] These veterans may feel irritable, on guard,

---

[18] Dave Grossman, *On Combat: The Psychology and Physiology of Deadly Conflict in War and in Peace* (Human Factor Research Group, Inc., 2011). Kindle edition.
[19] http://www.ptsd.va.gov/public/pages.ptsd-and-relationships.asp.

jumpy, worried, or nervous. They may have problems with relaxing, with intimacy, with flashbacks, etc. In addition, veterans may struggle with anger, tendencies toward anger, drug and alcohol problems, and a host of other issues. Thus, establishing the strength and support provided by strong relationships is essential.

A study of former child soldiers in Nepal suggests that separation creates major problems in one's life. Evidence for this appears in a 2012 article in *The New York Times*. Since 2006, Dr. Brandon Kohrt, a psychiatrist and medical anthologist at George Washington University, has followed the fates of Nepalese children who returned to their villages after serving with the Maoist rebels during their country's 1996–2006 civil war.

> All 141 in the study, 5 to 14 years old when they joined the rebels, experience violence and other events considered traumatic, aside from their separation from family. Yet their postwar mental health depended not on their exposure to war but on how their families and villages received them. In villages where children were stigmatized or ostracized, they suffered high, persistent levels of post-traumatic stress disorder. But in villages that readily and happily reintegrated them (usually via rituals or conventions specifically designed to do so), they experienced no more mental distress than did peers who had never gone to war. The lasting harm of being a child soldier, it seemed, arose not from war but from social isolation and conflict afterward. This finding is echoed in studies of American soldiers returning home: PTSD runs higher among veterans who cannot reconnect with supportive people and new opportunities.[20]

---

[20] David Dobbs, "A New Focus on the 'Post' in Post-Traumatic Stress," *The New York Times* (December 25, 2012).

We just completed a study of the importance of a faith community to our wholeness of life. It is within this community that God intended humans to demonstrate the dynamics of their transformed lives in interpersonal relationships.

The fact is that social isolation creates a major problem for many of our veterans returning from deployment in war zones. The good news is that God in his graciousness has provided a situation or community to address such isolation. This solution is a fellowship with others designed to provide strong relationships. Jesus' prayer to his heavenly Father for this community of people is as follows: I pray "for those who believe in me ... that they may all be one; even as thou, Father, art in me, and I in thee, that they may also be in us, so that the world may believe that thou hast sent me. The glory which thou hast given me I have given to them, that they may be one even as we are one, I in them and thou in me, that they may become perfectly one, so that the world may know that thou hast sent me and hast loved them even as thou hast loved me" (John 17:20–23). This community, which is designed to bring about such relationships, is called the church.

The apostle Paul pictures the church as a body of individuals called together to meet the needs of one another (cf. 1 Corinthians 12). The wise man speaks of the benefits of such relationship in this illustration: "Iron sharpens iron, and one man sharpens another" (Proverbs 27:17). Thus, we come together, and through such camaraderie, we meet the needs of one another, using our strengths to strengthen one another.

No matter how difficult it may be to admit, we must stay aware of the fact that we need others. None of us can claim to be self-sufficient. In fact, the Scriptures are filled with admonitions that are referred to as "one another" commands, commands that emphasize our dependence upon one another. We are to comfort one another (1 Thessalonians 4:18), build up one another (1 Thessalonians 5:11), confess to one another (James 5:16), pray for one another (James 5:16), and many other such admonitions.

The end result of this biblical emphasis on the importance of relationships is that we develop a wholeness and a more complete way of life. Within such a relational community, we sharpen one another, developing an ability to face with courage all that life may throw at us. As part of such a community, God will demonstrate the dynamic and the transformed life that he intended for us.

Who do you love and cherish the most? God did not intend for us to be alone, as seen in God's directive in Genesis 2:18, which says, "It is not good that the man should be alone." To avoid such loneliness, God provided us with many opportunities to develop relationships with our Creator, our family, and our friends.

The essence of being a believer in the Lord God and being a part of a community of believers is certainly more than adherence to doctrine, precepts, and commandments. Is not the foundation of the community of faith first and foremost a relationship? The Judeo-Christian faith was never meant to be a *religion* as it may be defined today. It was designed to be a relational community. Its aim was the establishment of an intimate personal relationship with our Creator. Yet we often face the tendency to go it alone, thinking we need no one. We tend to be misanthropic.

Whether we like it or not, the moment one decides to become a believer, he or she becomes a member of the *ecclesia* (*church* or *community*). We may refuse to identify with a church and share responsibilities with that community. We may even remove ourselves from it; however, we remain members, and such membership is essential to redemption.

So let us center our thoughts of three main relationships essential to a complete and wholesome life—the relationships with God, family, and friends.

Relationship with God

God never makes private, secret salvation deals with people, but he places us among other like believers. "The Lord added to their (believers) number day by day those who were being saved" (Acts

2:47). So the question is not "Am I going to be a part of a community of faith?" but "How am I going to live in this community?" God, who knows what I need better than me, sets forth the truth that I need community or relationship.

One thing we all have in common, however, is our fascination with relationships. We desire to fit in and to be accepted. We cannot wander through life alone, shut ourselves off from human contact, and expect to ever discover who we truly are.

What first comes to mind when we think of a relationship with God? In most religious traditions, typically we think of rules, rituals, regulations, and commandment obligations. In contrast to this, Scripture sets forth the truth that having a relationship with God is foremost and something very personal. In its formative stages, this begins the moment we realize our need for something or someone beyond ourselves, someone we can turn to in times of need. This is especially true when we realize we cannot walk through all the perils and challenges thrown at us alone.

The Scriptures teach that God exists and that he came into the world through Jesus Christ. Through Christ, he experienced every facet of life that we experience (cf. Philippians 2:5–8; Hebrews 4:14–16). Yet, do we have any real understanding of what it means to have a personal relationship with God, to trust in God, and to talk with God?

Do we believe that God truly desires to be included in our daily lives? The truth that he does care is clearly seen in Psalm 121. In verses 1 and 2 of this psalm, the psalmist asks and answers an important question, "Where is his help to come from?" Does it come from the ancient high places of pagan Baalism, which promised so much? In the same manner, where does our help come from when we are troubled or when we are trying to navigate through life? The world (modern-day Baalism) offers so many solutions. Are these solutions better than what God offers? Does the world offer the same genuine and personal interests in our welfare as does God? God is referred to by the personal name LORD six times in this psalm and is described as the keeper. He is not an impersonal executive that gives orders from on high. He is present with us in every step we take (cf. Psalm 139:1–12; Hebrews 13:5).

Why would we not seek a relationship with God? He is the very author and source of life. He never fails, never forgets, never compromises, never lies, and never disappoints. God's love is consistent, unwavering, unconditional, and unstoppable.

The Samaritan woman at the well (John 4:6–19) had probably given up on herself long before she had met Jesus. She had five failed marriages in her past, and she was even living with a man who was not her husband. As we read the narrative, however, we see that God had not given up on her. So in his providence, God opened up the opportunity for this woman to meet Jesus and to be restored in life. This same God is open and waiting for us to come to him. He will never leave or forsake us (cf. Psalm 118:5–9).

Relationship with Family

The typical veteran is very excited and elated about coming home from deployment. Yet many of these individuals who are returning from military tours in Iraq and Afghanistan encounter a significant adjustment as they reenter civilian life. The old adage "You can't go back home" is very true, for things are never the same as they were before you left. The veteran as well as the family back home have naturally matured over the months and have lived independent of each other. There is, of necessity, the work of reintegrating into each other's lives again.

Part of the adjustment following deployment is figuring how to reestablish relationships with family. Reintegration into the lives of family members involves taking time to become reacquainted with them. Open and clear communication is important for positive and supportive family relationships. Such involves listening to one another and restoring trust, support, and closeness. Many want families that are there for them and supportive of them. They want to return to or realize the American dream. They want to have that white picket fence and house. A growing body of research suggests that partners and close family members are essential and very beneficial to achieving that dream.

Relationship with Friends

An early Christian martyr once said, "A Christian's only relatives are the saints," those who share a mutual faith in God and his Son. In the same manner, veterans return home after sharing for many months a close bond with fellow veterans, a bond that is lost when they return home. The friends the veterans had prior to deployment have moved on in life, established new friends, and pursued their civilian goals and professions. They now seem more concerned with their pursuits rather than what the veteran experienced in war. So the veteran may find it easier to avoid trying to reconnect with former friends whose only interests may involve how many terrorist you might have killed or how many times someone shot at you.

As pioneers in early America moved west, each was given forty acres of land. At first they built houses in the middle of their land. Later, as more moved in, they built on the four corners closest to their neighbors. Why? They saw that the need for relationships was much more important than space and individualism. So the avoidance of former friends is not the solution to solving the need for relationships.

What is the veteran to do? The value and necessity of relationship with family and friends is extremely important. We have seen the necessity of such, but how do we go about facing and solving this issue. We will discuss this further in the next chapter of this book, "Facing Relationship Problems."

Chapter 5

Facing Relationship Problems

"Operational military deployment is stressful for military families. As of March 2011, there were 196,862 Active Duty and 54, 505 Reserve Component service members deployed in Operation Enduring Freedom (OEF) and/or Operation Iraqi Freedom (OIF). Of those currently deployed, 56% are married (140,546); 85% of married personnel report having children (96,976; and approximately 16% (15,832) of deployed personnel are single parents with at least one child."[21] What this data reveals is the essential value of giving more attention to post deployment family reintegration. Such is, in this writer's opinion, as important as facing issues such as veteran employment, mental health treatment, and physical rehabilitation, which are at the forefront in the reintegration of veterans into the family.

Reintegration into family life after returning from deployment often involves difficulties, for nothing is ever the same as it was before deployment. Further studies reveal that post-9/11 era married veterans faced more difficult times and problems readjusting to life

---

[21] Ramon Hinojosa, Melanie Hinojosa, and Robin S. Hognas, "Problems with Veteran-Family Communication during Operation Enduring Freedom/Operation Iraqi Freedom Military Deployment," *Military Medicine* 177, 2:191 (2012).

after deployment than veterans of previous wars. Overall, being married and being called away from home to serve the country reduces the changes of an easy reentry from 63 percent to 48 percent compared to the post-9/11 era.[22] The fact is that veterans in war zones tend to develop strong bonds with fellow soldiers. These bonds tend to function as substitute replacements for the ones shared with spouses prior to deployment.

We have previously noted that close relationships provide individuals with the most important meaning for their lives. In relation to this truth, shouldn't spouses/family be the most important source of comfort and support for post-deployment veterans? Certainly marriage is associated with a number of benefits, including better health, security, stability, and higher overall satisfaction with life.

Veterans of the post-9/11 deployment era were asked about the impact deployments had on their spousal relationships. Forty-eight percent reported a negative impact, underscoring the strain placed on married veterans leaving the service to rejoin their families.

The initial days and weeks following homecoming from war can be filled with excitement, joy, relief, and a host of other feelings. Yet this is often followed by situations that produce negative feelings and emotions. Things may not always be the same as they were prior to deployment, or they may not as what the veteran actually envisioned. All of this is a normal part of readjustment, however, as the veteran transitions back to civilian life.

We have seen the typical homecoming scene for veterans as depicted on television screens across the nation—families waiting in a gym or hanger; flags, banners, homemade signs everywhere; hugs, screams of delight, kisses, etc. These things are followed by neighborhood barbeques and "welcome home" parties. But is *reintegration*, a military term that has come to mean, "Let's cohabit and raise these kids," really this simple and easy? In reality, homecoming

---

[22] "The Difficult Transition from Military to Civilian Life." *Pew Social and Demographic Trends*. October 14, 2013.

is almost like a new marriage. It involves a period of adjustment. What is really involved in making two people into a couple again?

Soldiers don't have to worry about IEDs (improvised explosive devices), mortar attacks, or patrols. They are safe from these. Yet for spouses who remain home, there is a wide-range of emotions—relief that the loved one is safely back, guilt, anger, fear, even resentment. People change during long separations, and these changes are produced by the following things:

- Soldiers may have experienced traumatic events or injuries.
- Soldiers have lived in a culture completely different or foreign to his family.
- Soldiers separated from his friends in deployment.

In the life of a typical soldier on the battlefield, they look upon the enemy as an animal. They shoot him if he or she attacks. Poverty is rampant. They see the best and worst of humanity.

Once a Marine rescued an Iraqi's son and brought him safely home. The father was so grateful that he offered his daughter in marriage. How do you turn down that cultural tradition without offending someone?

A veteran in one of my university classes, who served as a military policeman said, "Prior to war, rare were domestic calls of abuse. Now there are many. We often have to confine a veteran in the barracks for seventy-two hours for cooling off. Some are like bulls, enraged for the bullfight."

At home major events take place. Babies are born. Funerals happen. New jobs are started. Households move. There are school events for kids. These bonding experiences are lost except for a short phone call and e-mail. Spouses at home have to learn to make decisions alone.

These things can make reintegration a challenge. Mood swings are common. The independence and intrinsic strength that enable one to cope with the lonely separation of war can become a wedge after deployment ends. The resulting period of adjustment and the feeling of distance between two people is normal, and it will take time to feel natural together again. The Defense Department reports divorce among soldiers on active duty has greatly increased and that 38 percent of marriages fail within six months.

Consider these two problems that veterans face in relation to recovery programs: (1) reluctance to admit they have a problem and (2) a lack of trust of the government, especially the Veterans Administration, with their private lives.

Veterans also experience difficulty in speaking to others. At war they learn to communicate with grunts, swear words, and sarcasm. These are simply ways they can cover up feeling confused or scared.

So what can we do to alleviate this situation both as veterans and spouses/families? Guidelines for reaching out are legion, but there are really no adequate, one-approach-fits-all solutions. However, the following pointers may aid in recovering relationships at home:

- Take time to relax.
- Be patient.
- Communicate.
- Be respectful.
- Plan a date night.
- Avoid excessive drinking.
- At times listen. Don't fix.

Other factors to consider in individual situations that can effect and improve the chances of easy reentry include the following:

- Consider your rank at the time of discharge. Commissioned officers are 10 percent less likely to experience difficulties.
- Veterans who clearly understood their mission were 77 percent (instead of 67 percent who didn't) more likely to have an easier reentry.

- College-educated veterans (78 percent) find reentry easier than high school-only graduates (73 percent).
- Those who attend weekly worship services are 24 percent more likely to have an easier reentry. In addition, they will have better physical and emotional health. These people are generally happier, and they have more satisfying personal relationships.

There are other considerations regarding domestic problems too. Make a list of changes you noticed when you returned home from deployment and how you addressed them. There are certain questions one must ask.

- Who am I now?
- What gives my life meaning?
- What am I thankful for?
- What is my relationship with my family and friends?
- How has my military experience affected my relationships?
- Are there ways I need to ask for forgiveness?
- Is there anything I want to change in my relationships?
- What do I regret?
- What do I fear?
- What makes me sad?
- What makes me angry?
- What is my source of strength?
- When do I feel spiritually alive?
- How do I want my friends and family to support me spiritually?
- How important is a faith community to me?
- What do I wish my spiritual leader to know?
- What spiritual sacraments or rituals are meaningful to me?
- What books, music, movies, art, other mediums are meaningful to me?

Chapter 6

Anger Management

In her book *Sparta*,[23] Roxana Robinson writes about the issues many veterans face during homecomings. In one story she speaks of US Marine Lt. Conrad Farrell, who comes home after two deployments in Iraq. While he is surrounded by supportive parents, siblings, and a wonderful girlfriend, he battles with rage over setbacks that might seem minor to others. Yet he tries to avoid help because, as a good Marine, he firmly believes he can handle these issues if he "sucks it up." In addition, for one who is seeking a spiritual relationship with God, there is this word from James in the Bible: "For the anger of man does not work the righteousness of God" (James 1:20).

Counselors report that 50 percent of counselees report problems dealing with anger, a malady that destroys relationships and communication, resulting in the ruin of the joy and health of those who are angry. Sadly, the tendency is used to justify anger instead of accepting responsibility for the outbursts. Anger and rage are prevalent emotions in individuals experiencing PTSD and obviously contribute greatly to the readjustment difficulties veterans suffer following deployment.

In relation to veterans and relationships, Dr. Edward Tick, author of *War and the Soul*, describes "the bond that develops between

---

[23] Roxana Robinson, *Sparta* (New York: Farrar, Straus & Girous, 2014).

people under fire together. The lives of those who share the mud and danger and blood of warfare become intermingled. The power of this bond transcends all others, even the marriage and family bonds we forge in civilian life ... Brother-in-arms or sisters-in-arms become liken to souls having one identity."[24]

The anger of warriors is often used to avoid the intrusive thoughts and emotions that come with intimacy and vulnerability. The warrior's thinking goes like this: *If I stay angry, I don't have to deal with those unwanted feelings.* Typically the veteran is angry for several reasons, but two primary ones include (1) the loss of friends along with the uncertainty of having lived in a totally random, unpredictable environment and (2) feelings of betrayal on the battlefield or the lack of power to complete an assigned mission.

Thus, anger becomes a source of power and energizes the angry party. These individuals perceive family members as easy targets. They need to control the environment, so when they sense they are walking into unknown territory, their emotions flare.

The following dialogue and information on anger is taken from the book, *Anger: The Misunderstood Emotion,* by Carol Tavris:

> A spouse speaks to her mate: "Honey, you would feel better if you get your anger out." The mate responds: "Anger? Why should I become angry?" "Because you have just returned home from deployment and things are not like you expected them to be and you are angry at everything and everyone." "What are you talking about? I don't feel angry. I feel sad and maybe disappointed." The first spouse responds: "Why are you denying your true feelings?" The other spouse replies: "Honey, you are going to drive me crazy. I don't feel angry, damn it!" "Then why are you shouting?"[25]

---

[24] Edward Tick, *War and the Soul* (Wheaton, IL: Theosophical Publishing House, 2005), 141–142.

[25] Carol Tavris, *Anger: The Misunderstood Emotion* (New York: Touchstone, Simon & Schuster, Inc., 1984).

One of the most accepted myths of popular psychology is as follows: "Expressing anger is crucial to health and happiness." Social psychologist Leonard Berkowitz of the University of Wisconsin states that advocates of this view believe it's unhealthy to bottle up feelings. They argue that by expressing our emotions, we eliminate tensions, conquer aches and pains, and promote "more meaningful relationships with others."

Psychiatrist John R. Marshall of the University of Wisconsin in the department of psychiatry writes that there is a widespread belief that discharging one's feelings or *ventilation* is beneficial. Furthermore, there is some value in hitting, throwing, or breaking something when a person is frustrated. But is this true?

The ventilation theory supposedly works like this: When someone or something irritates you and provokes you over the edge, you respond. You swear, hit, or pound out Stravinsky on the piano. All these reactions lessen your physiological arousal and its corresponding sensation that your blood is boiling. At the same time, you're acquiring a cathartic habit.

This doesn't mean that you will be less angry in the future. It means that when you are angry, you are apt to do whatever worked for you before, whether it was swearing, writing a nasty letter, having a drink, self-medicating, or yelling at or hitting the person who aroused you.

In contrast to this approach, "He who is slow to anger has great understanding, but he who has a hasty temper exalts folly" (Proverbs 14:29). The fact is that *any* emotional arousal will eventually simmer down if you just wait long enough. This is why the classical advice for anger control (e.g., counting to ten) has survived for centuries.

In his studies on social aggression, Dr. Berkowitz finds that ventilation, by yelling as an example, does not reduce anger. He has discovered that such activity stimulates continued aggression. This is why a minor annoyance, when expressed in a hostile language or behavior, often flares into a major argument. Often we react by punching holes in the wall, slamming doors, and so forth. This merely adds to our anger, and we become angry at ourselves for not maintaining better control. We may hate what we have become or what we are doing to a loved one.

Anger and its expression do not exist in a vacuum. In all areas of our lives, we make choices about how to behave, when to speak, and when to reveal anger. Suppressed anger can be bad if we fail to reveal our feelings and allow a stressful situation to continue. On the other hand, expressed anger can be bad if we reveal our feelings in ways that make the stressful situation worse or if we allow our anger to attack the wrongdoer and not the wrong done.

Anger can be very destructive power. There are those who believe that war is the greatest threat to humanity, but I believe it is anger. World War I left the nation of Germany in shambles and the people of Germany bitter toward the entire world. That anger eventually led to World War II.

What are some of the things we need to be aware of as we fight against the harmful effects of displaying a wrong kind of anger?

- We must demonstrate civility. We ought to use every measure we have to avoid being hostile or impolite to another. This is not the same as being silent.
- We must learn when to keep quiet about trivial angers and when to talk about and discuss important ones. Sometimes we need to let something go, for it will often turn out to be unimportant and quickly forgotten. On the other hand, anger is often inflamed by statements we make when we are provoked.
- Recognize the possibility that talking through anger may not get rid of it or make you feel less angry. Studies reveal that talking out an emotion may merely *rehearse* it and build more anger.
- Use "humor therapy."

The Department of Veterans Affairs has submitted a model on anger management called "An Anger Management Intervention

Model for Veterans with PTSD."[26] In this model, the report states, "Two key components to the successful application of anger management intervention for the veteran with PTSD are responsibility and accountability and the use of study logs."[27] The report sets forth a survey of the study and how veterans might conduct themselves to deal with anger management.

We must realize that anger can be a natural, normal, and honorable response to mean-spiritedness, injustice, and wrongdoing. In fact, as seen in the following Scriptures, such anger, which we label "righteous anger," is equated with being like God and Christ: Numbers 11:1–2, 2 Kings 17:17, Isaiah 5:18–25, John 2:14–17, and Mark 3:1–5. In fact, believers are commanded to be angry but avoid prolonging such. "Be angry but do not sin; do not let the sun go down on your anger" (Ephesians 4:26).

There is an anger that is sometimes called righteous anger, and it is manifested as a response against injustice, mistreatment, insult, or malice. In Christian circles, this is the only kind of anger that is not sinful. Biblical examples of such righteous anger are as follows:

- David's anger over hearing Nathan the prophet sharing an injustice in a parable (2 Samuel 12),
- the psalmist's anger over the sinfulness of Edom and Babylon against Judah (Psalm 137:7–9), and
- Jesus' anger over merchants and money changers defiling the temple (John 2:13–18).

Finally, this brings up the question of how to handle anger biblically. Whether fighting for moral values or even reacting from fleshly anger, what steps must we consider in handling such? How

---

[26] http://www.ncptsd.va.gov/publications/cq/v6/n3/gerlock.html?printable=yes.
[27] Ibid.

can we harness the power of anger and use it in godly ways? I suggest three basic approaches.

- We can recognize and admit that some of our anger is prideful and thus sinful, for we often mismanage or rationalize our anger.
- We can see that God may be at work in the particular trial that is making us angry, and we can realize that nothing happens that God does not cause or allow. Sometimes trials come to discipline and mature us (1 Corinthians 10:13; Romans 8:28).
- We can return good for evil (Romans 12:14–21; Matthew 5:43–48).

The famous Jewish psychiatrist Victor Frankl was stripped naked before the Gestapo. When a Gestapo officer demanded that he remove his wedding band from his finger, Frankl said to his captors, "There is one thing you can never take from me and that is my freedom to choose how I react to whatever you do to me!" Years later, recalling this, Frankl said, "What's the difference between human beings and animals? Human beings are not driven like a herd ... we can make decisions, we have a choice! That's what it means to be human."

Chapter 7

Overcoming Fear and Anxiety

According to the May 18, 2013, issue of *Science Daily*,

> Chronic trauma can inflict lasting damage to brain
> regions associated with fear and anxiety. Previous
> imaging studies of people with post-traumatic stress
> disorder, or PTSD, have shown these brain regions
> can over- or under-react in response to stressful
> tasks, such as recalling a traumatic event or reacting
> to a photo of a threatening face. Now, researchers at
> NYU School of Medicine have explored for the first
> time what happens in the brain of combat veterans
> with PTSD in the absence of external triggers.[28]

The results of PTSD greatly affect the fear circuitry in the brain.
An annual meeting of the American Psychiatry Association in San
Francisco revealed that "the effects of trauma persist in certain brain
regions even when combat veterans are not engaged in cognitive
or emotional tasks, and face no immediate external threats. The

---

[28] *Science Daily*. "For Combat Veterans Suffering from Post-Traumatic Stress
Disorder, 'Fear Circuitry' in the Brain Never Rests." May 18, 2013. http://www.
sciencedaily.com/release/2013/05/130518153257.htm.

findings shed light on which areas of the brain provoke traumatic symptoms and represent a critical step toward better diagnostics and treatments for PTSD."[29]

The report continues and points out that of the 1.7 million men and women who have served in Iraq and Afghanistan, an estimated 20 percent have PTSD. Further research has revealed that suicide risk is higher in veterans with PTSD, as more soldiers committed suicide in 2012 than the number killed in combat. Today hundreds of thousands of military personnel have seen combat and witnessed fellow soldiers killed or maimed, which may cause PTSD.

With this information before us, it is no wonder that many of our veterans face tough problems when they return home from deployment. Veterans often face a lifelong battle, and it is critical that they receive help, understanding, support, and encouragement whenever necessary.

Briefly, we are reminded again of some of the following facts about the development of PTSD, which can lead to fear and anxiety. The following are some facts about the development of PTSD:

- Women are more likely to develop PTSD than men.
- PTSD is often accompanied by depression, substance abuse, or other anxiety disorders.
- Fear and anxiety are not necessarily caused by combat wounds and injuries but by traumatic experiences relived through flashbacks, nightmares, and mental recall.
- PTSD may create a numbness in relationships to people with whom they used to be close.
- Flashbacks to the event(s) that caused PTSD are frequent.
- Suffers of PTSD may startle easily, be irritable and aggressive, and experience sleep disorders.
- Such trauma associated with fear and anxiety can persist in certain brain areas even when combat veterans are not

---

[29] Ibid.

engaged in cognitive or emotional situations and face no external threats (American Psychiatry Association).

- We must also recognize that fear-anxiety disorders are not just an experience or situation for veterans. The National Institute of Health reports that more than twenty-three million Americans suffer from some form of anxiety disorder.

One of the major questions facing Christians who are veterans concerns the use of tranquilizers and other mental health drugs to combat fear and anxiety from PTSD. Added to this is the popular teaching that fear and anxiety (worry) is a sin and reveals a lack of trust in God.[30] Worry comes from the Greek word *merimnao*, and it is a combination of two words, *merizo* and *nous*, meaning "to divide the mind." In reality, fear is an indispensable element in human makeup, and we should work to control and use it. We should not dispense with fear but face in the right ways. "Education consists in being afraid at the right time" (Angelo Patri, 1876-1965, Italian-American author and educator).

There is a difference between common anxiety and fear and that caused by PTSD. Common anxiety and fear need spiritual and psychological help, but seldom does it require mental health drug therapy. There is essentially nothing wrong with the brain's natural tranquilizers. Common fear and anxiety is mainly learned, and it has to be unlearned.

A common misconception is that tranquilizers are the main medications used to treat all anxiety disorders, leading to the belief that drugs *control* the mind and that they are addictive. The fact is that not all antianxiety medications are tranquilizers, and the risk of addiction is high mainly when such drugs are misused. The brain has its own tranquilizers (happy hormones), so tranquilizers are not foreign to the brain, and under normal situations, we are constantly producing these. However, fear and anxiety can rob the brain of its

---

[30] Here we distinguish the difference between *anguish*, which deals with the known, and *anxiety*, which deals with the unknown.

production of tranquilizers, and until the stress is removed, artificial tranquilizers may be necessary.

One of the major problems that veterans face in relation to fear and anxiety promoted by PTSD is *agoraphobia* (Gk. αγοϱφοβια). *Agoraphobia* (fear of the marketplace) is a situation where some are so fearful of messing up in an unsafe place that they refuse to leave the home. After all, Jesus says, "Do not be anxious" (Matthew 6:25, 34), and James follows by saying, "A double-minded man [is] unstable in all his ways" (James 1:8). Thus, a believer who worries is guilty of a sinful activity.

A holistic view of the Scriptures reveals that we must minister to people in distress, care for their lives, and lead them to a life promised by Jesus (John 10:10; cf. 1 Thessalonians 5:23; Philippians 4:7). This role includes assisting individuals with various disorders—physical, emotional, spiritual, and mental.

Listed below are seven suggestions that can be used to aid us in our personal development, but also in assisting veterans in developing stability in their lives as they acclimate into a post deployment life style.

1. Accept life's disappointments in stride without becoming unduly upset over minor problems.
2. Do not over or underestimate your own abilities and talents to solve life's problems.
3. You may be able to solve most problems in life, but do not be afraid to seek outside help when problems exceed your abilities.
4. Develop right attitudes in relating to others. Don't push others around, and don't allow them to push you around.
5. Accept life's responsibilities and face them. A person with a good attitude may say, "God grant me the serenity to accept the things I cannot change, the courage to change things I can, and the wisdom to know the difference."
6. Accept change, new ideas, and new experiences without feeling endangered.

7. Do your own thinking, and make your own decisions.

In no sense do we want to minimize the difficulties faced when we are confronted with fear and anxiety. Nor do we wish to offer simplistic ways to face such in our lives. However, I am convinced that only in establishing a relationship with our Creator will we promote a holistic lifestyle and be better enabled to handle the anxieties we face daily.

Carl Jung made the following statement about anxiety and fear: "About a third of my cases are suffering from no clinically definable neurosis, but from the senselessness and emptiness of their lives." I would put forth the biblical truth that establishing a relationship with the Lord God will fill the vacuum that is present in so many lives today. This action will reveal that faith is not simply a theoretical belief. No, it results in the development of a powerful trust and confidence in life as directed and lived in communion with our Creator, which results in better lives.

With these thoughts in mind, I offer the following suggestions that might find application in our lives:

1. Commit yourself to living the spiritual life, which involves
    - not trusting in your own ability to take care of yourself,
    - not seeking life directed only by the pleasure principle,
    - not trusting in material possessions, and
    - trusting in God and his Spirit within to guide you (1 Peter 1–5).
2. Live one day at a time. "Therefore do not be anxious about tomorrow, for tomorrow will be anxious for itself" (Matthew 6:34).
3. Refuse to violate your conscience, realizing that much of our anxiety comes from a failure to live by our God-given code of ethics.

Chapter 8

Guilt and Forgiveness

Many soldiers come back from deployment deeply wounded in spirit by the violence and evil of war. With a war that has been going on for more than a decade, there have been an unprecedented number of studies about the psychological effects on American soldiers, and most of these involve post-traumatic stress disorder (PTSD). Yet PTSD is not the total problem. There is also the problem of moral injuries—that is, involvement in situations that violate an individual's moral code. These are injuries that torture the conscience, resulting in a deep sense of shame and guilt. In studying the lives of veterans, the six most disturbing and presumably guilt-ridden experiences are as follows:

1) accidently killing other American soldiers,
2) seeing close friends and comrades killed,
3) seeing Americans killed,
4) placing bodies in body bags,
5) seeing atrocities committed against Americans, and
6) holding a friend as he or she was dying.

The most significant sources of guilt had to do with killing and death. Most of the soldiers in the American forces have been raised in a society that is adamant about killing. Jesus' ethic, "Thou shalt not kill," is deeply embedded within the American conscience. We may argue that this excludes killing for self-preservation or killing in a war zone, but still the moral side of taking a life raises its head time and time again. If you have been involved in such situations of killing, you may expect some of the following:

1) guilt from taking a human life, producing a strain on the conscience;

2) guilt from having lost moral values, permitting one to kill and to cause intense physical and emotional suffering for others;

3) guilt of having become hardened to the loss of life to the point of being without conscience;

4) guilt from being unable to control violent thoughts and behaviors;

5) guilt from feeling that you have turned from God and that you are becoming hardened spiritually; and

6) emotional and moral outrage, which urges many veterans to become the victims of alcoholism, drug addiction, antisocial behavior, and suicide.

Occupying the top of the list of guilt emotions is the so-called survivor's guilt. This is the emotion expressed when a fellow soldier is killed beside you and you are not hurt. This event is accompanied by thoughts that you could have or should have done something to prevent the loss of life, though in fact, you did nothing wrong. But how reasonable is this feeling?

Nancy Sherman has written the following:

> We often *take* responsibility in a way that goes beyond what we can reasonably be *held* responsible for. And we feel the guilt that comes with that sense of responsibility. Nietzsche is the modern philosopher who well understood this phenomenon: "*Das schlechte Gewissen,*" (literally, "bad conscience")—his term for

the consciousness of guilt where one has done no wrong, doesn't grow in the soil; where we would most expect it, he argued, such as in prisons where there are mutually "guilty" parties who should feel remorse for wrongdoing. In "The Genealogy of Morals," he appeals to an earlier philosopher, Spinoza, for support: "The bite of conscience," writes Spinoza in the "Ethics," has to do with an "offense" where "something has gone unexpectedly wrong." As Niezsche adds, it is not really a case of "I ought not to have done that."[31]

Thus, survivor guilt is caused by several factors, such as surviving while others have died, a feeling of invulnerability, feeling insensitive to being hurt, being involved in activities that have destructive effects on others, and even a failure to fulfill one's purpose (not winning the war).

There is, however, a positive side to survivor's guilt, for it imposes a moral order on the chaos and randomness of war's violence. It is a way to humanize war for all who are caught up in its evil. It is also a reflection of who we are in terms of character and relationships.

The big question concerning survivor's guilt involves the possibility for combat veterans to find guilt resolution and spiritual transformation through Judeo-Christian spiritual principles. Is there hope for recovery?

There are stories of transformation through seeking spiritual help, turning to God, and applying the spiritual principles set forth in scripture. Two such stories are as follows:

A Marine combat veteran suffered from a personality disorder before entering military service. Upon discharge, he developed the symptoms of PTSD and alcoholism, for which he sought psychiatric help but received little or no results. Then seven years after the

---

[31] "The Moral Logic of Survivor Guilt," *The New York Times*, "Opinionator," July 3, 2011, D2.

war, he had a Christian conversion experience that brought about a remarkable change in his life. His nearly broken marriage was restored, and his recurring traumatic dreams, attacks of rage, and alcoholism ceased to be problems. Furthermore, his sense of pervasive meaninglessness was replaced by a desire to help others. Since then, he has maintained a normal family life and developed a self-supporting spiritual ministry for helping people in need, particularly other combat veterans.

In another example, a former patient of the Bay Pines Stress Recovery Program left a hospital treatment program abruptly when he assaulted another patient. He later reported a Christian conversion experience nine months after discharge. His symptoms, prior to recovery, included rage attacks, nightmares, intrusive imagery, feelings of guilt, emotional detachment, alcoholism, flashbacks, episodes of disassociation, and feelings that his body was possessed by evil spirits. When he lying in bed one night, fearful of going to sleep, he described his situation, "I felt that if I went to sleep, the Devil would get hold of me and I'd wake up in hell. So I called out to my wife and asked her to pray for me. She did, and I asked Jesus to take over my life. Within one or two days, I began to get a sense of peace and a new feeling of self-control that I had during the previous fifteen years."[32]

The Bible is probably the most widely used reference that seeks to provide spiritual recovery, comfort, and directions. In fact, veterans are more likely to sustain their recovery when involved in a spiritual group similar to that of AA. Two excellent examples of the use of Scripture in facing guilt and isolation are as follows: Psalm 55:4–8 could easily come out of the experience of a veteran, and Psalm 60:1 clearly expresses feelings of alienation from God

Why is it that some veterans avoid spiritual help? Some studies reveal that it is primarily caused by an intense anger at God. The

---

[32] Joel Brenda and Elmer McDonald, "Post-Traumatic Spiritual Alienation and Recovery in Vietnam Combat Veterans," *Spirituality Today* 41, no. 3 (Winter 1980): 319–340.

love of God, as revealed in 1 John for example, is incompatible with the kind of hatred war tends to unleash.

At this time we may want to examine the biblical concept of sin, those various acts that seem rebellious against God-established moral principles and perimeters, activities that can produce guilt. It is such violations (or supposed violations) that can and often do cause such guilt feelings within the lives of many veterans.

One of the major discontents of society is guilt. This guilt has been described also as a major cause of the loss of happiness within personal lives. To quote Hamlet, conscience "doth make cowards of us all." To address this situation, I have set forth the following exercises, and I encourage the reader to identify with and reflect on the Scriptures and what I have written in each exercise.

1) Read Genesis 3 and notice the areas of separation caused by sin (cf. Isaiah 59:2).

In the Genesis 3 creation story, the first couple was placed in the Garden of Eden to enjoy, among other things, fellowship with God (Genesis 3:8-9). However, the man and women yielded to the Tempter, disobeyed God, and brought into the world sin, misery and death. Thus, separation from what is good and true, which is the result of sin, became a reality in the life of humankind.

The kinds of separation brought about by the sin of Adam and Eve are as follows:

- Separation between God and humanity (Genesis 3:8, 23),
- Separation with neighbor (Genesis 3:15–16),
- Separation between humanity and nature (Genesis 3:17b–19),
- Separation within self (Genesis 3:7), and
- Separation between moral good and moral evil (Genesis 3:15).

This separation between moral good and evil is evident today when we resist the good that comes from the kind of life God intends for his people to live. When we violate the ethical principles of our faith, we are involved in resisting, grieving and finally quenching the promptings of God's Spirit within (cf. Acts 7:51; Ephesians 4:30; 1 Thessalonians 5:19), thus causing the kinds of separation listed above within our lives.

2) Define survivor's guilt.

Following the death or severe injury of fellow soldiers, veterans sometimes feel shock, responsibility for the event, or remorse for surviving. Individuals coping with survivor guilt may face questions such as the following:

- Why didn't I get hurt?
- Why did I live when others died?
- What could I have done to prevent such death of a soldier?

We recall that this kind of survivor's guilt is often unreasonable and irrational, because the guilty individual knows that he or she did nothing wrong. Character is not about what one has done or should have done but rather about what one cares deeply about. Of course, we are not saying that we don't have to "walk the walk" in right living, but we need to recognize that virtue is also concerned with emotions and attitudes. Here are four tips on coping with survivor guilt:

- Acknowledge your feelings and recognize they are normal reactions.
- Seek out others for support, and share your feelings with peers.
- Take time to mourn, or plan your own way to remember the victim(s).
- Turn your negative feelings into positive actions.

3) How would you respond to one who is experiencing survivor's guilt?

Recognize that it is possible to counterfeit things, twist them, and use them in destructive ways. Guilt is good at times, and it can let us know when we are doing something that is leading us to a separation from God and his will for us. When this happens, we can go to the Lord for forgiveness and restoration. However, false guilt can produce frustration, depression, and inner conflict. Survivor's guilt can often be associated with this kind of destructive inner conflict. Note the following comments:

- You can't blame yourself because you lived while others died. You had nothing to do with that. You cannot control all situations and events.
- The euphoria over your personal survival is an involuntary response, part of uncontrollable reflexes, not moral choices that you should be held accountable for.
- In hindsight, we may see other options we could have taken, but in the moment of crises and fog of war, you can't see them all. You did the best at the moment, and no one should judge you for it.
- Leaders simply can't protect all those under their command all the time. War is hell! The potential for death surrounds the combatant at all times.

In all situations like this, it is normal to feel sad, angry, and frustrated about how things turn out, but don't turn that emotion in on yourself. Do not allow unfortunate events to weaken and destroy you. Life isn't fair!

4) What advice would you offer someone seeking forgiveness from others he or she may have harmed?

In order to heal, each of us must receive forgiveness from both God and from others we may have hurt. This is among the most difficult things to do. However, we must admit the wrong we did to another and ask for forgiveness. Jesus gives this great truth in Matthew 5:23–24. Note the following:

- Ask God to show you who you have hurt (Psalm 139:24).
- Ask God to forgive you the pain you have caused others. This is really a double sin, for you have sinned against God and his child. We must first confess and repent to God.
- Pray for the one you have hurt. This entails asking God to heal the wound you have inflicted. Then pray that the person is open to your plea for forgiveness and does not feel hostility toward you.
- Take the initiative and go to the one you have hurt. Here again, you must plea with God for the courage to take this necessary step.
- In humility, recount to the person what you did and ask for forgiveness. Do not try to minimize the deed or cast yourself in a better light. You cannot take the spotlight off your responsibility and shift it elsewhere.
- Work on rebuilding trust with the individual you have hurt. This will take time and effort. It will require demonstrating that you meant what you said.

5) Why should we seek to forgive those who have harmed us?

We should forgive for the sake of Christ. 2 Corinthians 5:17–18 reveals that God is recreating the world through disciples of Christ. We should forgive for the sake of others. God does not love and forgive us because we repent. Rather we repent because God loves and forgives us (cf. Romans 5:8). Reconciliation is the task of the victim. We should forgive for our sake. The parable of the unforgiving servant (Matthew 18:23–35) reveals that we are forgiven as we forgive. Forgiveness is the key to liberating us from a painful past and opening our eyes to a new future.

Chapter 9

Regaining Faith

After experiencing many of the horrors and difficulties of war (being wounded, losing fellow soldiers, the uncertainly of what the next step on patrol might mean, engaging the enemy in fierce combat, separation from loved ones and family, etc.), many come back home and realize that the great longings we now have in our lives are not being fulfilled by churches, synagogues, and other institutions.

Yet many veterans realize as well that they are more spiritually-oriented than they thought. At the very core of being human, we find that humans are spiritual beings. We realize that the great religious truths of our past traditions are more desperately needed than ever before. There is also a God who has survived all the onslaughts of the world, and he remains alive and necessary. Even if we concluded there is no God, we have to admit that *we wish there were one.*

Veterans come back home, seeking material possessions and luxurious living. Yet there remains a deep hunger for more. This is primarily due to the fact that the life of the Spirit is alive in our hearts, whether we admit it or not. This deep hunger is expressed so well by the early church father, Augustine: "We were made for you, O God, and our hearts are restless until they rest in you" (Augustine of Hippo. 354-430 in *Confessions*).

Humans are religious. We all seek something higher than ourselves to worship. Deep within all of us is that which goes beyond us and moves us to connect with humanity and the universe. There remains a transcendent dimension that we might call the Deity.

We believe in God, experience his influence in our lives in a thousand ways, desire to celebrate his existence, and yearn to celebrate his presence from time to time. So why don't we just go to church and do these things? Why don't we engage in the great hymns, hear and say the prayers of the faithful, and listen to the ancient words?

The fact of the matter is that *many veterans do not. Why?* They may have grown up in churches and attended churches in their premilitary days, and yet they do not find the spiritual hungering and nourishment in churches and the rituals that they experienced in the past and so desire now.

In 2014, I began a work with post-deployment veterans in a church in Nashville, Tennessee. This group met on the first and third Sunday afternoons at this church building. The purpose of the formation of this community of veterans was set forth in the following statement, which also reveals much about how the veterans feel about organized religion:

> The purpose of this community is to develop a safe and supportive environment as we strive to be transformed by our Lord Jesus Christ. Our desire is to make this community Christ-centered, yet non-churchy. The community presently meets the 1st and 3rd Sundays of each month. We plan to address veteran-related issues, spirituality, transition to civilian life, etc., while engaging in community service projects. In addition, we hope to be supporters of one another in spiritual development and accountability. There will also be planned recreation and fun activities, identifying resources pertinent to veterans, the invitation of guest speakers, attention to our families, and studying God's word together, all within an informal and relaxing environment.

Several things stand out in this statement of intent. These veterans express a deep desire to maintain a spiritual component in their lives as seen in the importance of Bible study and spiritual development. They also manifest a concern for family, community involvement, and accountability to God, neighbors, and themselves. Notice also that there is a concern that reflects a kind of negative attitude toward the church as an institution. This is revealed in the statement in remarks made about this newly-formed community of veterans being "nonchurchy" and being in "an informal and relaxing environment."

Obviously, churches have difficulty in reaching such individuals. Scores of books have been written about this situation, and *churches do want to reach out* to those who are struggling with such faith issues. Yet something remains missing. Something is wrong. I feel empty. I go to church and make no connection. My spirit is not fed. I am bored more often than uplifted.

To address these needs, many have turned away from organized religion, seeking other organizations and practices that promote peace and tranquility, yet they still feel spiritual. While finding no help in structured religious ritual and assemblies, they still feel the need for faith in their lives.

Scripture informs us that God desires his people to reach out to these individuals living on the margins of the society. The world can be a troublesome place for many of our veterans, and when they feel they must "go it alone," they become even more vulnerable. This is why it is essential for churches to get involved in the lives of the veterans. The Lord wants us to be his voice, his ears, his hands, and his feet to the marginalized so that they might have a place of refuge and peace, a sanctuary in this post-deployment world. This is who God's people are and what our churches are called to be.

In my experience with veterans, I have seen that there are basically three different approaches they take as they seek some kind of spiritual empowerment not found in their experience with organized religion.

First, there are those who seek no religious life at all. While many choose this path, it is very difficult to eliminate all religious phenomena because spiritual realities are present in the subconscious of every living person.

Second, these are those who seek a master and sit at his or her feet, symbolically or actually. These people engage in meditation, yoga, and chanting exercises. They hope that through such experiences they will be able to express their religious longings, study religious teachings, and improve their lives.

Third, there are those who join a semireligious group that has goals and ritual practices that fit their individual goals and feelings. It is natural to desire to join some group that will accept and support you. The larger question before us is this: "What are we looking for?"

When the subject of healing our spiritual life or regaining faith comes up, we usually think of doctors. After all, doctors do something to bring about healing. They set bones, give some antibiotic, remove some diseased part of the body, and prescribe some medicine to assist in overcoming some mental or psychiatric disorder.

But are these professionals really healing us, or are they adjusting our environment in such a way that the normal healing process that God has built within us can proceed unhindered?

Reflecting on this situation, how might we be able to provide some insight? It might be that we can apply some *medicine* to our lives that will allow us to recover a spiritual life that includes regaining the faith that used to sustain us in our previous years. Of course, this will not happen overnight. After all, we have not arrived where we are now in a single evening. What we can do, however, is deepen our connection with the spiritual and to the Lord God so that he can accomplish his healing work within us.

I think the place to begin this journey is Psalm 91, which says, "He will cover you with his pinions, and under his wings you will find refuge … You will not fear the terror of the night, nor the arrow that flies by day, nor the pestilence that stalks in darkness, nor the destruction that wastes at noonday." Really? Is the psalmist correct in saying that I need not fear the things that now plague me in my daily living? Is there possibly a level of faith that can honestly produce such a way of life even after all allowance has been made for poetic exaggeration? Can faith and participation in faith activities (worship, prayer, Bible reading, etc.) help alleviate the pain and disorder that has come into our lives?

In response to this question, researchers at McLean Hospital, a psychiatric institution affiliated with Harvard Medical School, asked 159 patients with prominent symptoms of depression how strongly they believed in a god.[33]

They also asked how credible the patients thought their treatment was and how effective they believed it would be in relieving their symptoms. The patients' symptoms were assessed when they were admitted and again when they were release from the program.

Seventy-one percent reported believing in a god or a higher power to some extent. Those who possessed a faith system that they felt was deep and strong, regardless of their god or religious affiliation, were twice as likely to respond well to the treatment and experience a better outcome than those without a strong spiritual base. The researchers point out that people who believed in a god or were associated with a religion were also more likely to believe their psychiatric treatment was credible and to expect positive results.

"It may be," they reported, that "the tendency to have faith in conventional social constructs can be generalized both to religion and the medical establishment. Since other studies have shown that faith in a given treatment is an important predictor of its effectiveness that could help explain the association with the improved outcomes found here."[34]

In 1993, only three of the 125 medical schools in the United States offered any sort of course work exploring the area of spirituality and medicine. Today more than ninety of these medical schools have formal courses where they explore randomized controlled

---

[33] http://articles.mercola.com/sites/articles/archive/2013/05/09/can-faith-in-god-help-alleviate-depression?.
[34] Ibid.

studies and the effects of spiritual practices on longevity and health outcomes.

"The correlation between spiritual practices and health outcomes is just too strong … For example, the data shows that people who follow some sort of spiritual path in their life live on the average seven to 13 years longer than people who do not follow a spiritual practice … We have a huge spectrum of data that shows, I think compellingly, that your thoughts really matter when it comes to getting well."[35]

Where do we begin this journey that takes us back to faith? Two things are needed. First, we need to know the laws, and second, we need to obey the laws. These laws do not include expected things. We do not say, "Go to church three times a week, carry a Bible with you all the time, bathe in holy water, and live a perfect life." The laws have to do with developing a deeper relationship with God, cooperating with his healing process, and giving him access within us to heal. The Scripture set forth certain God-ordained principles and laws that will optimize the healing process.

Primary in this healing process is the promised Holy Spirit or Comforter as a helper. Jesus gave the assurance of this holy presence to his disciples prior to his crucifixion, resurrection, and ascension into heaven (John 14:18–27). God's healing process begins with us allowing the Holy Spirit to dwell within us—that is, by receiving the Holy Spirit. The Holy Spirit's task is to live within us, empower, heal, and enable us to live righteous and satisfying lives.

Read the following biblical passages and reflect on what they tell us about our desires to live whole, satisfying lives, ones realized through this indwelling power called the Holy Spirit:

- John 14:16–17, 26–27—In this section, take note of the emphasis on the Holy Spirit and his function as a strengthening companion who will teach and empower. In addition to

---

[35] Larry Dossey, *Healing Words: The Power of Prayer and the Practice of Medicine* (New York: Harper Collins Publishers, 1994).

teaching and reminding Jesus' followers, we find the promise of peace (*shalom* in Hebrew, meaning "wholeness of life"), the kind of peace that Jesus possessed and displayed in his life.

- John 16:13—The guidance promised by the Holy Spirit here is that believers will be given the ability to lead a successful and complete way of life that will sustain them in the life to which Christ calls them.

- Acts 1:8—The believer is here promised the ability to carry on the work of Christ in the world as a witness and a source of enlightening and leavening influence in the community (cf. Matthew 5:13–16).

- Romans 8:26–27—The Holy Spirit supports and helps the believer so that he or she may endure faithfully, even in the midst of moral weaknesses, until the final day of redemption. He creates within us high and worthy goals and then empowers us to realize such goals.

When the Holy Spirit comes into the Christian's life (i.e., when he indwells within the believer), he is not going to force himself on us. As Scripture informs us, we can resist, grieve, and quench the Holy Spirit's influence within our lives (cf. Acts 7:51; Ephesians 5:30; 1 Thessalonians 5:19). However, the Spirit can and will guide and direct us in life-giving ways *if* we allow him to do so.

In addition to the previously outlined passages, read, reflect, and find encouragement in the following biblical instructions in relation to God's or the Holy Spirit's work within us as we strive to live faithfully:

- Ephesians 5:18—The world seeks to face difficult situations in life through drugs and alcohol. The Christian is reminded that successful living is promoted by possessing a clear mind with the inspiration and guidance of the Spirit of God.

- Matthew 5:6—When we realize how painfully deficient we are in acquiring the necessary things that lead to life and godliness, then we will turn to God and find fulfillment or satisfaction, which will result in peace (cf. Romans 5:1).

- 1 John 1:9—Living as Christians means that we are aware that sin is a continuing problem in our lives. The good news, however, is that we do not have to deny that we sin or fail to live up to our expectations. We have continuing forgiveness and purifications based on God's love, justice, and faithfulness to our highest welfare.
- Romans 6:13, 16–19—Here, the believer is challenged to fight against the evil powers of the world that often beset us. God will free us believers from all manner of evil forces that try to enslave us.
- Luke 11:9–13—Living in the world drives the sincere individual to his or her knees in prayer. Jesus urges his disciples to have great confidence in prayer. God will deal with loss, disappointment, and tragedy in the lives of his followers. And once again, we have the assurance of the Holy Spirit in these situations.
- Mark 11:24—Prayer and the expression of prayer is the way we can display our hearts' wishes to the heavenly Father. By God's compassion and deliverance, he will, without failure, develop within us the kind of life and character he designed for us.

To sum up this chapter on regaining faith, we come to the realization that we need to entrust our lives to our heavenly Father, who will never fail or forsake us (cf. Hebrews 13:5b). And this faith or trust does not mean that we just believe in a set of doctrines and exercise right rituals. Rather it mean entrusting our lives to him and seeking his will and purpose in all that we do. When we do this, we will turn to him and see that he will supply every need and that he is sufficient for whatever problem may come our way. When we turn to him in faith and trust in his power, then we will find life.

Chapter 10

Prayer

One serious concern in early America expressed the need for prayer in the life of the US military soldiers and their families. In the early days of this nation, one of the principles of the Continental Navy approved by the Continental Congress in November 1775 reads as follows: "The commanders of the ships of the Thirteen Colonies are to take care that divine service be performed twice a day on board, and a sermon preached on Sundays."

On July 9, 1776, General George Washington noted in his orderly book that the Continental Congress voted to allow each regiment in the newly formed nation's army a chaplain, and he also expressed his hope that "every officer and man will endeavor to live and act as a Christian soldier, defending the dearest rights and liberties of his country."

From the American Revolution through the War of 1812, the War between the States, World Wars I and II, and beyond, the American soldier and their families, communities, and citizens back home have turned to prayers at crucial moments. President George W. Bush declared at a National Day of Prayer gathering in 2001, "Our country was founded by great and wise people who were fluent in the language of humility, praise and petition. Throughout our history, in danger and division, we have always turned to prayer.

And our country has been delivered from many serious evils and wrongs because of that prayer."

Our soldiers have experienced so much violence and so many threats as they are deployed around the world. The ever-present specter of pain and death creates so much turmoil in the lives of our soldiers as well as the lives of their families and loved ones back home. Following such life-altering experiences, veterans come home from deployment and face equally challenging situations as they acclimate back into the society. This makes it vitally important that they become men and women of prayer.

In spite of General William Tecumseh's famous Civil War speech and his well-known words that war "is all hell," there is the positive aspect that war sometimes produces good things, such as love of country and kin, sacrifice, courage, and comradeship. In addition, war often raises spiritual awareness and creates a greater reliance on God's grace, comfort, and protection. Many veterans voice their convictions that prayer releases God's power, protection, and presence in their lives wherever they are serving and in whatever situations they find themselves, both foreign and domestic. In a survey of more than sixteen thousand active-duty soldiers, *The Journal of Alternative and Complementary Medicine* reports that prayer is the most common "alternative medicine" (CAM) used by the military.[36] Realizing the importance of prayer in the veterans' post-deployment efforts, it is necessary, therefore, for us to spend time examining prayer and questions we might have about this subject. As a good starting point, we can pose and respond to several points often raised when we consider prayer.

The supreme importance of prayer is tacitly admitted by most Christians, yet there are a few areas of the Christian life in which there are more regrettable confessions of failure and disappointment. Therefore, it is essential that we strive to know where we are on the

---

[36] Kim Tippens, Kevin Marsman, and Heather Zwickey, *The Journal of Alternative and Complementary Medicine*, April 2009, 15 (4): 435–438. Doi:10.1089/acm.2008.0480.

scale of prayer knowledge. Six statements along with an additional thought are listed for consideration and reflective response.

1) Define prayer in your own words. As the disciples, we need to pray, "Lord, teach us to pray" (Luke 11:1).

2) Is God a prayer answerer or a Father? Do we desire a father who gives us our every request or one who responds to our requests in ways that reveal love and concern for our highest good?

3) If God already knows everything, why pray? Are we informing God as if he doesn't know or inviting him into the situation to assist us in our journey?

4) The only real answer to prayer might well be the strength to be weak in the world. Could the apostle Paul have been right when he spoke in relation to his thorn in the flesh and responded, "My grace is sufficient for you, for my power is made perfect in weakness" (2 Corinthians 12:9)? The good news set forth here is that all the obstacles faced in life, obstacles that empower our weak resources, drive us to the all-sufficient power of Christ. Human weakness and inadequacy in the midst of seemingly overwhelming obstacles is the best possible situation for the display of divine power. The apostle Paul's glory in his weaknesses is due to the security of his faith in the complete adequacy of Christ to lead him into triumph through the power of Christ within, not the power of self.

5) What are some obstacles to prayer? Obstacles to prayers vary in each individual's life, but some of these can include tensions between faith and reason, the problem of evil in the world, some great personal loss, among others. These things are a challenge; however, in the midst of such, recall these words: "Thou dost keep him in perfect peace, whose mind is stayed on thee, because he trusts in thee" (Isaiah 26:3).

6) What if God does not answer your prayer? Consider the old adage, "God gives us what we need, not what we want."

James adds, "You ask and do not receive, because you ask wrongly" (James 4:3).

Realizing the importance and effectiveness of prayer in so many lives and situations, we ask now about the characteristic of acceptable prayer. After all, if we engage in prayer, we ought to have some idea as to what is required of acceptable prayer. Reflect on each point in the following list and your personal conclusions about prayer.

1) Prayer must be offered in faith (Matthew 21:22; James 1:6–7). Maybe we need to offer the same petition to God that the man offered in relation to Jesus' ability to heal his son. "I believe; help my unbelief" (Mark 9:24).

2) Prayer must be offered in sincerity. In 1 Corinthians 14:15 Paul speaks of the importance of praying with full consciousness ("with the mind"). Prayer is designed for edification, thus the necessity of prayer in genuine sincerity. The Greek word for sincere literally means "without wax." The Greek sculptors would often cover the flaws in their statues with wax to make them appear more perfect. Could it be that I often try to cover the flaws and imperfections in my life when I speak with God in prayer? Or maybe in Paul's situation with the church in Corinth, trying to impress God and others with my finesse in prayer?

3) Prayer must be offered with understanding (Romans 8:26–27). Am I truly thinking about the words that I use so that the words may become my words, or am I uttering trite and worn out phrases, thinking people will hear me if I use many words?

4) Prayer must be preceded by faithful living (Proverbs 28:9; Romans 12:1; 1 Peter 3:10–12; 1 John 3:21–22). The life I live and the prayers that I offer must not be in contradiction with each other. Avoid vain repetitions (Matthew 6:7–8). Does God answer requests because of the number of times we recite a certain phrase?

Acceptable prayers must include the following elements:

1) They must include adoration and praise (Matthew 6:9; 1 Chronicles 29:11; Psalm 104:1; Jeremiah 32:17; Jude 24–25). When we come before our awesome God, we cannot but adore and praise because "worthy art thou, our Lord and God, to receive glory and honor and power, for thou didst create all things, and by thy will they existed and were created" (Revelation 4:11)

2) They must include thanksgiving (Luke 17:15–18; Psalm 107:1; Colossians 4:2; Philippians 4:6). Pray in the knowledge that in spite of the present darkness, there always remains promise and possibilities.

3) They must include confession (1 John 1:9). Not only does prayer reveal the honest truth about the self, but it is also accompanied by an intention to change with God's help.

4) They must include petition (Matthew 6:11–13). While prayer should not be for the self alone, it certainly is acceptable that we petition for guidance in our journey and help in becoming what God desires us to be. "Lord, teach us how to pray," is often a phrase we hear. However, in reality, the apostles requested, "Lord, teach us *to* pray" (Luke 11:1; cf. Matthew 6:9–15). This request was not about *how* to pray but simply *to* pray. We often get so bogged down in the how that we forget that we only need *to* pray.

Realizing the importance of prayer in the believer's life, we turn to the Lord's Prayer, the model prayer, found in Luke 11. When the veteran is reaching out for real and lasting values in life and searching into the deepest mysteries of life and self, prayer often comes to the forefront. We find ourselves asking, as did the disciples of Jesus, "Lord, teach us to pray." Luke 11:1-13 is our Lord's most comprehensive lesson on prayer.

In this model prayer, notice the details and characteristics that stand out as basic concerns for any prayer. Read each section below and reflect on how these comments may assist you in your prayer life. This will be important as we strive to develop our personal prayer life when we petition God's help when facing situations in life which tend to overpower us. I

- "Our Father"—We can approach God in prayer as children in a very intimate and personal manner. Approaching God in earnest faith and reverence is essential, but also in the consciousness that he is our Father who is near us in mercy and love. We approach God with the rights of a son. All that a father ought to be to his children, God is to us.

- "Hallowed be your name, your kingdom come, your will be done, in heaven as on earth"—The glory of God's name, the coming of the kingdom, and God's will is set forth in this petition. The more our prayers conform to these particular concerns (i.e., God's glory, God's kingdom, God's will), the more fully will he occupy his rightful place in our hearts and lives and the more effective our prayers will be.

- "According to your will"—We may wonder if this is a kind of inhibiting condition to prayer; a kind of fine print at the bottom; a requirement that prayer must be in his will or it will not be effective. In reality, when we pray, with the will of God as our primary desire, then this will release us from our deepest concerns about life because it assures that the will of God surely will be carried out. And what is this will other than God's desire for our highest good?

- "Give us day to day our daily bread"—Praying this aspect of the Lord's Prayer helps us to realize our utter dependency upon our heavenly Father for every blessing and gift in relation to our lives on earth. This text indicates that all of our concerns are important to God. If he is concerned with the lily of the field and the sparrow (Matthew 6:28), how much more is his concern for us? God is the God of the macrocosm and the microcosm, the infinite and the infinitesimal, the universe as well as the smallest part of creation – the atom.

- "Forgive us our sins; for we also forgive everyone who sins against us"—Believers must be willing to forgive, and this becomes a key factor in healing relationships that have been broken for various reasons. The importance and value of the community is realized only when that relationship is built on the principle of reconciliation with God and others. The true Christian community is a reconciled and a reconciling community, and this is where its power lies (Matthew 18:15–35; 1 John 4:20).

- "Lead us not into temptation"—Seeking and entreating forgiveness for wrongs against God and others recognizes the longing to sin no more. So, we must always be praying that we be given the opportunity to avoid any situation that might cause failure. We can never be presumptuous about temptation. We cannot use God's love, forgiveness, grace, mercy, and long-suffering as a license to sin.

- "Ask, and it will be given to you; seek, and you will find; knock, and it will be opened unto you" (Luke 11:9–10). In Mark 11:24, the writer adds something of importance to prayer: "Whatever you ask in prayer, believe that you will receive it, and you will." The assurance of answered prayer is grounded on God's faithful commitment to us, that being, his desire for our highest good.

- "If you then, who are evil, know how to give good gifts to your children, how much more will the heavenly Father give the Holy Spirit to those who ask him" (Luke 11:13). The basis of God's part in prayer is vividly set forth here. If our earthly fathers naturally give us the best they can give, how much more will our Father in heaven give in response to our petitions? Here is the promise from God: "I will give you my best!"

Chapter 11

Depression and Suicide

Exposure to combat trauma is one of the most common and the single best predictors of PTSD and depression. This creates expensive mental disorders, costing the United States an estimate $66 billion annually. A Rand study estimates that 320,000 veterans have experienced brain trauma (2008).

"Clinical depression is a serious medical illness that is much more than temporarily feeling sad or blue. It involves disturbances in mood, concentration, sleep, activity level, interests, appetite, and social behavior. It is highly treatable. But frequently a lifelong condition" (National Alliance on Mental Illness).

Veterans account for 14 percent of the total number of individuals experiencing depression, one in three suffering from this disorder. Yet only about half report their problems because they fear documentation will harm their careers. This situation reveals the importance of the VA and military organizations providing confidentially. Seeking help is a sign of strength, not weakness.

Studies also reveal that veterans struggling with depression are more likely to commit suicide or battle substance abuse than non-veterans. Males are three times more likely to commit suicide than females. Caucasians are at higher risk than African-Americans and Latinos. Further studies reveal that females have higher rates of depression than males.

Interestingly, PTSD suffers are less prone to suicide than those not diagnosed with PTSD, possibly because PTSD sufferers are more prone to seek psychiatric care, and thus have access to diagnosis. As pointed out earlier, clinical depression is more than some temporary feeling of sadness or despondency. It involves disturbances in mood, concentration, sleep, activity level, interests, appetite, and social behavior.

Some of the most common symptoms of depression are:

- persistently sad or irritable mood;
- pronounced changes in sleep, appetite, and energy;
- difficulty in thinking, concentrating, and remembering;
- physical slowing or agitation;
- lack of interest in or pleasure from activities that the person once enjoyed;
- feelings of guilt, worthlessness, hopelessness, and emptiness;
- recurrent thoughts of death or suicide; and
- persistent physical symptoms that do not respond to treatment, such as headaches, digestive disorders, and chronic pain.

One veteran reported, "Over there (deployment), I never had the time, energy, or free will to even begin to deal with some of the emotions I was bottling up. A few months after I got back was a different story, though. I was finally having to deal with all the issues I'd stored away."

Studies reveal that although major depression can be a devastating illness, it is highly treatable with success rates of 80 to 90 percent. On the other hand, untreated and undertreated cases result in cascading sets of consequences—drug use, suicide, marital problems, unemployment, etc.

While medication and psychotherapy have been proven effective for depression, *group support* from fellow veterans is very effective in overcoming depression. There are a number of effective treatments for depression that can lead to positive and meaningful changes in symptoms and quality of life.

Hundreds of thousands of veterans have gotten help, and *treatment works!*

One veteran reported, "I wasn't a big fan of pills, or therapists for that matter. But I got to the point where anything was worth a shot. Now that I got the treatment I needed and see how much better every day looks, I wish I would have gone sooner."

Many studies have determined that individual treatments for depression may include the following:

- Walk, jog, or work out.
- Eat healthier and regularly.
- Get a good night's sleep.
- Practice relaxation or grounding techniques like cognitive thinking.
- Try volunteer work and community service.
- Identify with a Christian community that educates people about the purpose, laws, values, and attitudes that produce *shalom* (wholeness of life).

Many veterans experience depression with its accompanying feelings of inadequacy and unworthiness. This is a medical condition that has been developing for a long period of time, so treatment will require time to make lasting progress. Therefore, it is imperative that the sufferer considers the following: First, recognize that you have not chosen a depressive lifestyle and would gladly give it up if you could. Second, love and acceptance make up the foundation for recovery. Too often the depressed person has heard someone say, "Snap out of it. Quit feeling sorry for yourself. It's all in your head. Pull yourself together." These people need understanding, not advice.

The Problem of Guilt

In relation to guilt, it is feasible that individuals may feel guilty for some moral failure in the past. This does not mean that the depressed person is guiltier than others but that his or her experiences may have made the individual oversensitive to failure. It is important here that we deal with the distinction between *real guilt* and *pseudo guilt*. Real guilt is the conviction that one has violated some ethical or moral value (see the David and Bathsheba story of 2 Samuel 11–12). Pseudo guilt is the feeling of unworthiness and inadequacy stemming from past experiences, which may not have been in any way the fault of the individual suffering from false guilt. It is a psychological mechanism, such as experienced with victims of survivor's guilt.

The best way to deal with pseudo guilt is by understanding the fact that the guilty individual is turning feelings of hostility (anger at enemy soldiers, anger at person who brought some bad against him/herself), toward self, not others. It's not that the individual necessarily could have done anything to change things, either. So, how does one overcome the desire to turn the feeling of guilt toward oneself when such is not merited?

Here I have listed three things guilt-depressed individuals typically feel at one time or another. Read and reflect each of these and see if they fit into your situation, and determine what if anything you can do to assist your own or another's situation

- Depressed individuals fear rejection. These individuals are afraid that others are not interested in them. These individuals think that acceptance is conditional, that it is based on what they do or don't do. One must live up to a certain standard to be accepted. In reality, such individuals need to experience love and concern. One way to handle this is to educate yourself in the grace and mercy of God, to enjoy the abundant life offered to one who believes (John 10:10). It would be helpful to concentrate on the words of the Apostle Paul in Philippians 4:8.

- Depression is, in pseudo-guilt situations, often due to wrong values, desires, and attitudes, and it is brought on by one's desire to punish self by developing a "get me" attitude (an attitude that promotes self-punishment) rather than accepting God's love and grace. The solution often offered, that being, to commit to avoiding the violation of God's spiritual and physical laws is often dead-end for it is too easily coupled to a pattern of being overly rigid, conscientious and perfectionistic. The issue is not so much what the individual thinks, but what God promises in the way of freedom from such attitudes through his grace, mercy and forgiveness, that is essential to remember and emphasize.

- Depression is also caused by an overestimation of one's value. Studies reveal that many people who are depressed have not recognized and accepted the fact that we are all sinners, unworthy to stand before God, as seen in Isaiah 6:5. A solution may be realized by balancing any feelings of inadequacy with the readings of Psalm 8:4–5 and Matthew 22:39, in addition to other passages with themes of hope.

Augustine of Hippo (354-430 in *Confessions*) states, "Thou hast made us for Thyself and our hearts are restless until they rest in Thee." A major reason for my depression may be that I am trying to live outside of a relationship with God. Several individuals are interested in ways of reaching out and making a difference in the veteran's life. Consider these four directions if you desire to help depressed individuals.

- Maintain normalcy as much as possible in the relationship.
- Point out distorted and negative thinking without being critical or disapproving.
- Communicate love, care, and acceptance with all the power you can muster.
- Try to keep the depressed person busy and active physically, while trying to encourage good dietary habits as well.

As reported here, depression is one of the most common and expensive disorders in the United States, especially among post-deployment veterans. In 2013, for example, the US Department of Veterans Affairs released a study that reported on suicides from 1999 to 2010. The study revealed that about twenty-two veterans per day were taking their own lives through suicide.[37] In relation to US military deaths, note the following chart:

TABLE 1: SUICIDE RATES BY SERVICE (2001-2010)

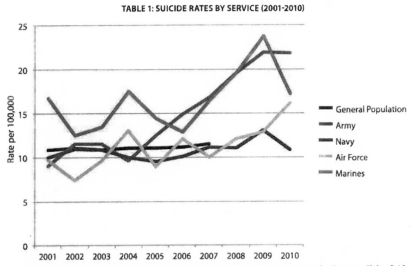

Sources: All data represent active duty suicide rates. Army 2001-2002, Air Force 2001-2003 and Marine Corps 2001-2005 data are from Department of Defense Task Force on the Prevention of Suicide by Members of the Armed Forces, *The Challenge and the Promise: Strengthening the Force, Preventing Suicide and Saving Lives* (August 2010). Army 2003-2010 data are provided by the Army Health Promotion and Risk Reduction Task Force. Navy 2001-2010 data are from the Navy Personnel Command website, http://www.public.navy.mil/bupers-npc/support/suicide_prevention/Pages/HistoricStats.aspx. Air Force 2004-2010 data are from "Air Force Long Term Active Duty Suicide Rates" (August 12, 2011), AFSPP Manager of the AFMSA/SG3Q. Marine data for 2006-2010 rates were obtained from a telephone conversation with a Marine Corps representative, September 7, 2011.

US Military Deaths

The occurrence of suicide dates back as far as recorded history. Suicide is even described in Egyptian, Hebrew, and Roman ancient writings. It was discussed by Greek philosophers, and it remains a vital concerns of authors, physicians, psychologists, and theologians, to name a few. The Bible records seven suicides—Abimelech (Judges 9:53–54), Samson (Judges 16:28–31), Saul (1 Samuel 31:1–6), Saul's

---

[37] "U.S. Military Veteran Suicides Rise, One Dies Every 65 Minutes," *Reuters* (February 1, 2013). Retrieved on May 23, 2013.

arms bearer (1 Chronicles 10:4–5), Ahithopel (2 Samuel 17:23), Zimri (1 Kings 16:15), and Judas Iscariot (Matthew 27:3–5).

While murder is clearly prohibited in the Scriptures (Exodus 20:13 states, "Thou shalt not kill"), there is no direct evaluation of suicide, although suicide may be considered self-murder. This action is a sin against God, the Creator and Sustainer of life, for he alone has the sole right to take a life in accordance with his divine sovereignty. Human life is God's sovereign gift.

Suicide is the act of intentionally and voluntarily taking one's life. Suicides fall into two types, conventional and personal. Conventional suicides occur as a result of tradition and the force of public judgment. Some instances include Japanese men of rank stabbing themselves when facing disgrace (called *hara-kiri*), Indian widows being forced to immolate themselves by cremation on the funeral pyre of their husbands, the old and infirmed being exposed to the element in certain primitive tribes, among others.

Personal suicides are more typical of modern times, and these are on the increase. There were 28,100 recorded suicides in the United States in 1981. It is estimated that for every suicide, fifty to a hundred more are attempted but unsuccessful. Despite gains over poverty, rising living standards, and progress in battling pain and disease, suicide rates in the United States continue to rise and do so even among younger and affluent persons.

The process by which a person arrives at the decision to take his or her own life is not easily analyzed. By the time there is a case for analysis, the individual is dead. The general theory is that a person commits suicide because he or she is unable to adjust to the stresses and strains of life. Others feel that this act signals a withdrawal from some intolerable situation. Others see it as a symbolic murder, whereby the people who commit suicide identify themselves with people they hate. Thus, by killing themselves, they are symbolically killing those they abhor. At the same time, these people ease their conscience in the anticipation of their own punishment, namely their execution (by suicide) for wishing to murder others. It seems best to view suicide as a way to solve various problems—loneliness, hate, desire for revenge, fear, physical pain, feelings of guilt, and so forth.

Various factors may influence individual attitudes toward suicide and affect the frequency with which people resort to taking their own lives. The following facts allude to some interesting matters pertaining to these influences.

Religious convictions may influence individual attitudes toward suicide, but such convictions are rarely conclusive, for some countries reveal high suicides among one religious group, while another country reveals low suicide rates among the same religious groups.

Age also affects suicide rates, as evidence reveals there are fewer suicides among the very young and the very old in comparison with middle-age people. A 1971 study published in a statistical bulletin of *Metropolitan Life* shows a decrease in suicides at ages fifty-five and older, and in fact, there's also a small decrease in people between forty-five and fifty-four. It is important to realize, however, that this data does not lend itself to a precise analysis due to several contributing factors which influence the data, such as, the present state of the economy, the increase in healthy life expectancy, the prevalence of substance abuse in the society at any given time, improved medical support services, and so on. What the data does do, however, is to call attention to possible trends in suicidal rates in various age groups thus providing another parameter in determining the suicide risk among various individuals.

In most countries men commit suicide more often than women. Women, however, make more unsuccessful attempts at suicide than men. Professional people with relatively high educational levels (doctors, dentists, lawyers, psychiatrists, etc.) commit suicide more frequently than those with lower educational levels. It is interesting that suicides are significantly higher among psychiatrists than among those working in any of the other sixteen specialty groups listed by the American Medical Association as a part of the medical profession.[38]

Suicides vary in response to economic conditions. If the years are prosperous, there are fewer suicides than there are during periods of depression or recession.

Many have often said that the man who threatens to take his life will not actually carry this threat out. This is not true, however, for approximately 75 percent of the people who do commit suicide give definite warnings of their intent.[39] Some who speak of suicide do not actually attempt to end their lives, but their threats should not be ignored. Suicidal people use the announcement of their decision as a cry of help. If the act of suicide is a desperate cry for help, then the announcement of its impending possibility should be taken seriously in all cases. The reality of the emotional disturbance does not depend on whether or not these people actually attempt to take their own lives. Regardless of their words, they still need help. Their threats to "end it all" are signs that they are dissatisfied with life and are experiencing feelings of rejection and unworthiness.

Every individual who is engaged in counseling or helping people will confront the problem of suicide and suicidal attempts. The range of severity will vary from the threat of suicide, which is often used to gain attention, to the successful suicidal act. Regardless of whether these people are serious in their threats or not, such threats are an indication of emotional disturbance and must be addressed.

Louis Dublin, a pioneer in suicide prevention, once remarked that the peer counselor is "probably the most important single discovery in the fifty-year history of suicide prevention. Little progress was made until he came into the picture."[40] This statement reveals the importance of nonprofessionals in the area of suicidal counseling and also reveals the need to give such individuals all the knowledge

---

[38] *Bulletin of Suicidology* (Washington, DC: US Government Printing House, December 1968), 5.

[39] "Patterns of Disease," Parke, Davis and Company (May 1963).

[40] L. I. Dublin, "Suicide Prevention," in E. S. Shneidman, ed., *On the Nature of Suicide* (San Francisco: Jossey Bass, 1969).

possible so they can determine and help the suicide-oriented person. The counselor's task will be twofold. He or she must judge how serious the threat to take one's life is, and the counselor must take some kind of positive action in the situation.

In order to judge how serious a threat of suicide is, the helper must be able to recognize and evaluate some of the clues that the potentially suicidal person offers. Collins points out that there are generally five such clues.[41] Sometimes these clues are very subtle and require alertness on the part of the counselor. We should consider these potential clues at this time.

- Verbal clues—These clues are of two types. There's the vocal threat used to gain sympathy, and then there are the more subtle types that follow such statements as, "I won't be at work next week" or, "I won't ever be able to do this again." It is appropriate at times to inquire about someone you might suspect of being suicidal if he or she has ever thought of taking his or her own life. If the person is able to give details, chances are that suicide is a very real possibility. Some individuals with suicidal tendencies may even approach the counselor and ask, "What can I do about a friend who is contemplating taking his own life?"
- Behavioral clues—It is possible to see definite changes in a person's behavior when he is contemplating suicide. The psychologist Wayne Oates writes that prior to a suicidal person's definite decision to take his or her life, "the person may be depressed, experience frontal headaches, and be joyless by day and sleepless by night. After a decision has been made, there may be a period of waiting for the actual perpetration of the act. At this time, the person may seem suddenly quite serene, happy, and moving about setting his life back into order after a time of immobilization and illness.

---

[41] Gary Collins, *How to Be a People Helper* (Santa Ana, CA: Vision House, 1976), 102–05.

The experience clinician will not be fooled by this dramatic, seeming recovery. Instead, double attention is given and even considerable initiative will be taken in alerting relatives and friends close to the person to stay near the person in this critical span of time."[42]

- Descriptive clues—In the opening words of this chapter, we discussed some of the various factors that can influence individual attitudes toward suicide. Things such as age, health, gender, and economic conditions are clues that may reveal the suicidal tendencies of individuals. For example, if a young person speaks of suicide, it may not be as real a threat as, say, a middle-age professional in poor economic straits. In this latter situation, careful attention needs to be paid.

- Situational clues—The basic factors underlying suicidal thoughts center upon feelings of desperation and dissatisfaction with life. The person who considers taking his life is an unhappy individual who sees no purpose or meaning in life. He feels that the only way to escape his continual feelings of worry, despair and depression is to end his life. Such feelings can be caused by poor health, terminal diseases, loss of job, divorce, loss of a loved one, and so forth.

- Symptomatic clues—Shneidman says that there are several symptoms that can indicate that a person is not coping with stresses well. These include depression, hopelessness, disorientation, confusion, complaining, dissatisfaction, and even a defiant attitude. One with this attitude may say, "I may be down, but at least I'm in charge of ending my life when I please." Alcoholics, drug users, and people with terminal illnesses are high on the list of likely suicides. Many take their lives to escape unpleasant situations, such as terminal illnesses, or in the case of alcoholics and drug users, they commit suicide to inflict and sustain punishment they believe is merited.

---

[42] Wayne E. Oates, *The Psychology of Religion* (Waco, TX: Word Books, 1973), 195.

A final topic we will address in this chapter is the prevention of suicide. One study revealed that two-thirds of all suicidal persons communicated their intentions before taking their lives, but the people who received the communications either panicked or did nothing. [43] This reveals the necessity of being able to recognize suicidal persons and then being able to respond with concern and positive assistance. Frederick and Lague give some much-needed and helpful advice in this matter, as seen in their research

Which follows:

1) *Do* take seriously every threat, comment or act. Suicide is no joke. Don't be afraid to ask the person if he is really thinking about committing suicide. The mention won't plant the idea in his head. Rather, it will relieve him to know that he is being taken seriously, that he is better understood than he suspected.

2) *Don't* dismiss a suicidal threat and under-estimate its importance.

3) Never say, "Oh, forget it. You won't kill yourself. You can't really mean it. You're not the type." That kind of remark may be a challenge to a suicidal person. Such a person needs attention, not dismissal. Anyone desperate enough can be "the type."

4) *Don't* try to shock or challenge the person by saying, "Oh, go ahead and do it." Such an impatient remark may be hard to hold back if a person has been repeating his threats or has been bothersome to have around. But it is a careless invitation to suicide.

5) *Don't* try to analyze the person's behavior and confront him with interpretations of his actions and feelings during the moment of crisis. That should be done later by a professional.

---

[43] E. Robins, J. Gassner, J. Kayes, R. H. Wilkinson, Jr., and G. E. Murphy, "The Communication of Suicide Intent: A Study of 134 Consecutive Cases of Successful (Completed) Suicides," *American Journal of Psychiatry* 115 (1959), 724–733.

6) *Don't* argue with the individual about whether he should live or die. That argument can't be won. The only possible position to take is that the person *must* live.

7) *Don't* assume that time heals all wounds and everything will get better by itself. That can happen, but it can't be counted on.

8) *Do* be willing to listen. You may have heard the story before, but hear it again. Be genuinely interested, be strong, stable, and firm. Promise the person that everything possible will be done to keep him alive, because that's what he needs most.[44]

The Christian helper has a divine source of strength and wisdom to help people. Because of the interest and concern a Christian counselor shows to individuals, many have turned from despair and rejection and embraced purposeful living in the reality of Jesus Christ. Our Lord assured us with these words: "I came that they may have life, and have it abundantly" (John 10:10). Life in Christ is worth living. As Christian helpers, we must get this message to others.

---

[44] C. J. Fredrick and L. Lague, *Dealing with the Crisis of Suicide*, Public Affairs Pamphlet No. 406A, New York, 1972.

Chapter 12

Discovering Peace (Shalom)

Shalom is a Hebrew word meaning "peace, completeness, prosperity, and welfare." It can be used idiomatically to mean both hello and good-bye. In English, it can refer to either the peace between two entities (as between God and man or between two countries) or to the well-being, welfare, or safety of an individual or a group.

In Hebrew, the root of the word *shalom* has several meanings. For example, it can also mean wholeness or completeness. The word *shalom* ("peace") is common in other languages (*paz* (Sp); *paix* (Fr.) *pace* (Lt), *pax* (Latin), and *irene* (N. T. Gk). While this word can mean truce or treaty, a relationship activity, a state of mind or affairs, or quietness and rest, this certainly does not limit its meaning to just these definitions. In the Hebrew and Greek Scriptures, the word *peace* refers to a state of mind, being, or affairs. Equally true, the word is not limited to just a state of life, but also freedom from the threats and results of war.

Derived from the Hebrew, *shalom* seems to encapsulate a reality and hope of wholeness for the individual within every societal relationship. On a more abstract application, *shalom* points to welfare (e.g., health, prosperity, and peace). *Shalom aleichem* is a greeting that states, "Well-being be upon you," or, "May you be well," a greeting equivalent to hello.

Consider the following:

> The webbing together of God, humans, and all creation in justice, fulfillment, and delight is what the Hebrew prophets call *Shalom*. We call it peace but it means far more than mere peace of mind or a cease-fire between enemies. In the Bible, *Shalom* means universal flourishing, wholeness and delight—a rich state of affairs in which the natural needs are satisfied and natural gifts fruitfully employed, a state of affairs the inspires joyful wonder as its Creator and Savior opens the door and welcomes the creatures in whom he delights. *Shalom*, in other words, is the way things ought to be.[45]

The writer of Ecclesiastes reveals his solution to developing *shalom* in one's life when he says, "Fear God and keep his commandments for this is the whole *duty* of man" (Ecclesiastes 12:13). The word *duty* is in italics in the previous quotation because this word was not in the Hebrew text but was added by translators. The literal translation says, "Fear God and keep his commandments for this is the whole person" (cf. Jesus in John 10:10).

General William Tecumseh Sherman, Union general in the Civil War, was right when he said, "War is hell," as any veteran would know. War is a profound life-changing experience, the ultimate violence, and it changes military men and women like nothing else does.

Unable to cope with life after war, many suffer from depression, abuse drugs or alcohol, become angry and irritable, have trouble sleeping, and suffer from PTSD.

As discussed earlier in this book, PTSD includes two basic types of symptoms. The first involves experiencing the event again

---

[45] Cornelius Plantinga, *Not the Way It's Supposed to Be: A Breviary of sin* (Grand Rapids, MI: Wm. B. Eerdmans Publishing Co., 1995).

and again, which can occur as flashbacks, nightmares, or thoughts that enter the mind. The second involves focusing on avoidance to minimize the pain, which may consist of avoiding people, places, or things that remind the individual of a particular event.

So desiring *shalom* and possessing *shalom* are two different things, and this difference forces us to ask, "How do we obtain *shalom?*"

First, I think we must start with the wise man of Proverbs, who says, "As a man thinks in his heart, so is he" (Proverbs 23:7 KJV). This mentality is often referred to as "imaging," picturing vividly in your conscious mind a desired goal or objective and holding that image until it becomes a regular part of your thinking. If you firmly imagine the kind of individual you wish to become, that is the person you ultimately will become.

If you think that you can fail or might not be able to encounter such a goal, failure will stalk you no matter what. The universe is like a great echo chamber. Sooner or later what you send out will come back to you. If you love people, that love will be reflected back (Leviticus 19:18). If you sow anger and hatred, anger and hatred will be what you reap. If you concentrate on yourself and your own problems, people will not be drawn to you. If you have a certain mental picture of yourself, you will become that picture.

In Kowloon, Hong Kong, Norman Vincent Peale saw a tattoo shop and was fascinated with the various designs in the window. As he was shopping, the owner came out and talked with him. Peale was especially fascinated with a tattoo that said, "Born to Lose," and he asked who would want that tattoo. The Chinaman said that he had placed that on the chest of a man just last week. "Why on earth such a gloomy tattoo?" replied Peale.

The old man said, "Before tattoo on chest, tattoo on mind."

There are three deadly emotions that can rob a person of self-esteem and promote inferiority—fear, guilt and doubt. Let us now consider these in great depth.

Fear

An ancient Russian proverb states, "A hammer shatters glass but forges steel." What does this mean? Sometimes fear can destroy one's confidence. One may withdraw from the society. In that case, the person may not possess the faith to cope with hardship or uncomfortableness.

Yet others are forged into stronger individuals in the face of adversity. How is this possible? I think fear can be overcome through trust. "Fear not for I am with you ... I will help you, I will uphold you with my victorious right hand" (Isaiah 41:10).

What did we do as children when we were caught in a major storm? We ran to our parents' bedrooms; however, they didn't turn away, and they didn't make fun of our fears. Rather they offered love and support until the danger was past. This is our Lord's promise to us: "Lo, I am with you always, to the close of the age ... I will never fail you nor forsake you" (Matthew 28:20; Hebrews 13:5).

Guilt

This image-damaging emotion is very real in the lives of veterans, especially for those who faced combat situations and saw innocent lives lost or friends killed in action. How can you possibly think well of yourself if your own conscience condemns you?

In his novel *The First Circle*, Alexander Solzhenitsyn described a prisoner who obsessively marked a pink sheet of paper for every bad thought or defect. I have known people who have gone through life with this hyperactive attention to defects. They often feel there is no hope for them. Martin Luther would wear his confessors out with as many as six hours of introspection about his guilt. One of his advisers finally said, "My son, God is not angry with you. It is you who is angry with God." I read a caricature of a Puritan as "a person with a haunting fear that someone somewhere is happy."

So what do we do if we feel a false guilt? Examine the accusation. Is God condemning me, or am I condemning myself? If we have violated God's will or other people, we should feel guilty and thank God for his forgiveness. We must allow our guilt to point us back to the offense and then move torward repentance.

True guilt only serves its purpose if it presses us toward God, who promises forgiveness and restoration. Martin Luther learned later in life that one cannot live sinless, so he said, "Sin and sin boldly." He meant that to live is to sin, but he also understood that we should not allow sin to cripple us. Rather, we should live courageously and realize that God is forgiving us at every moment (1 John 1:7).

Phantom guilt is an ugly thing that consumes our minds and saps our strength. It is a lingering guilt for something you should no longer feel guilty about. You've beaten yourself up enough for the guilt to last for two or three lifetimes. God wants you to feel okay about moving on. Either the cross was good enough to pay for your sins, or it wasn't. Phantom guilt does not come from God, and it's not going to undo the past (Jeremiah 31:34; Hebrews 8:12; 10:17).

Doubt

This is the third great stumbling block to *shalom* and confident self-imaging. It is perhaps one of the greatest enemies of faith. Maybe we need to pray that old Scottish prayer that says, "Oh, Lord, give me a higher opinion of myself." Is this arrogance … or conceit? No, it isn't. Matthew 22:39 instructs us to love others as we *love ourselves*. We should be aware of our potential and move forward with assurance and confidence, an assurance and confidence that comes from the Lord in us (cf. Psalm 8). When our minds are weakened by doubt, we have a strong tendency to exaggerate the size of the difficulties we face. We need only to recall that favorite childhood story of *The Little Engine That Could* when we face fears that we are not capable of handling threatening situations that confront us.

Nine Ways to a Better Self-Image

How do we think about ourselves? Our response to this question will have an effect in every area of our life, for good or for ill. When we possess a positive self-esteem, we feel joyous, exuberant and happy. We will enter into new situations with optimism and confidence and typically will accomplish what we set out to accomplish. We will face moments that are frustrating and problematic; we will take on new responsibilities; yet we can face these challenges without being overwhelmed. Why? Because these are the general consequences of possessing a positive self-image. Therefore, if this be true, how do we gain insight into developing a positive self-image? I offer the following nine suggestions to reflect on and strive to apply to life:

1. See yourself always as a child of God (Romans 8:31). To live a victorious life, one hardly needs more to know than that God is desirous for our success in every area of life.

2. Stand in front of a mirror and take a good look at yourself. Check your external appearance (posture, clothing, etc.) and then your inner self. Your appearance goes a long way toward helping you to achieve goals and objectives because you are what you feel, see and act. In addition, your appearance determines, to a large extend, how others react to you.

3. Decide to improve your capacity for imagining. Picture the best and not the worse happening to you. Actualize yourself, and you will improve. The wise man wrote: "For as he thinketh in his heart, so is he" (Proverbs 23:7, KJV). The mind is powerful. We ourselves determine, to a large extent, what we become. This is just another way of saying that what we visualize, in the sense of a better future or outcome, will ignite a drive within that will assist us in realizing what we desire.

4. Practice what you do well, and learn success. This builds confidence, whereas dwelling on the lack of success destroys confidence. Learn to do what you do well.

5. Condition your conscious mind with spiritual power principles: The Apostle Paul's great principle of life was in his conviction that he could "do all things in him [Christ] who strengthens" him (Philippians 4:13). Once again, we emphasize the truth that there is a great source of strength available to all men and women of faith.

6. Sensitize yourself to the beauty, variety, and excitement of living. Life is filled with marvelous gifts—family, friends, art, literature, nature, universe, discoveries—and we are a part of all this. Studies reveal that one aspect of low self-esteem is its tendency to isolate the individual from society. Yet, a life of gratitude for what surrounds us in the community moves us to become more prosocial and more satisfied in life.[46]

7. Control your emotions. Emotional stability is, in fact, one of the strongest predictors of contentment and life satisfaction. This, in turn, leads to higher self-esteem.[47]

8. Stay close to Jesus Christ always. He is the same yesterday, today, and forever, and he will never leave you or forsake you (Hebrews 13:8; 13:5; Philippians 4:4–8). Sometimes we begin to doubt our value and worth as an individual. In the midst of such difficult times, when we wonder how we will come through them, the promise of Christ will never fail. We are never alone.

9. Pray for peace. "Let the peace of God rule in your hearts, to which indeed you were called" (Colossians 3:15). We can find inner peace by filling our minds with scripture and with the presence of the Holy Spirit. The Apostle Paul assures us, "that according to the riches of his [God's] glory he may grant you to be strengthened with might through his Spirit in the inner man....Let the word of Christ dwell in your richly" (Ephesians 3:16; Colossians 3:16).

---

[46] Michael McCullough, Shelley Kilpatrick, Robert Emmons, and David Larson, "Is Gratitude a Moral Affect?" *Psychological Bulletin*, Vol. 127 (2) (March, 2001): 249-66.
[47] Peter Hills and Michael Argyle, "Emotional Stability as a Major Dimensions of Happiness," *Personality and Individual Differences*," Vol. 31, Issue 8 (December 2001): 1357-64.

Chapter 13

The Veteran and College

The influx of veterans entering college raises the major issue of whether campus officials are meeting the needs of this unique student population. As veterans reintegrate into the routines of civilian life, we should pay special attention to easing the transition process and providing a supportive environment.

Do you as a veteran feel that you often have to deal with the issues alone, issues such as educational benefits, the complexity of college requirements for the education offered, ways to transition more effectively to college life, etc.?

If you are suffering from symptoms of PTSD, experiencing war trauma, stress, impairments of one kind or another, or even wondering if you can succeed in college, do you feel you must suffer in silence? Do you feel that seeking or asking for help is a sign of weakness? What kinds of problems have you encountered as you have learned to function in an unstructured environment, such as college life, in contrast to the highly organized structure of the military world? What experiences have you had in relation to those who may have negative opinions against the war or even those civilians with the reverence for your service? What experiences have you had with professors and staff who just fail to understand the issues veterans face?

These situations bring us to the point when we must ask, "What is it like to go to college after serving in the military?" On the university campus, you will join fellow students who are possibly eight years younger than you are. However, you don't just have a new set of peers to grapple with. There are other issues.

Our military training was interactive and in the moment, but now you are completing reading assignments, writing essays and term papers, taking final exams, and other such matters.

However, the fact is that veterans have a great advantage over the younger student. For example, you have much more insight in dealing with stress and complex problems, and you are much more mature. You typically have greater maturity, discipline, motivation, and focus. So what kind of advice is there for veterans enrolling in college?

First, prepare for a transition. In the military there was always someone of a higher rank who told you where you needed to be that day. In college, however, you come to campus, and you are management. You determine what you need to do each day, and you discipline yourself to do it, whether it is studying, reading, or whatever.

Second, be open to a new mind-set. You cannot be standoffish and think about how dumb and stupid many eighteen-year-olds are. Veterans must be more open to hearing different and less mature opinions than theirs, and they must at least learn to hear these people out. Recognize that our students can greatly benefit from the experience and training you bring to this campus. You should also recognize that sometimes civilian students can feel uncomfortable talking to veterans because they don't know what is appropriate and what is off limits.

Third, seek out other veterans. It is very encouraging to meet and hear from other people on campus who are going through the same things. One of the challenges veterans face is missing the camaraderie from their fellow veterans. Veterans often learn best from those who have been where they were. The feeling of being unlike those around you can hamper life on campus. Seek fellow veterans who can offer support and understanding. This will lead to a much more fulfilling campus life.

Fourth, while this may sound like it runs contrary to what has been developed thus far, hang out with civilians. It is very important to broaden your horizons and actually get to know the civilians sitting beside you in class. You need to do things outside your veteran sphere. Become involved in campus life. Join fraternities. Participate in other social activities.

Fifth, avoid doing only online courses. Online courses may make things easier, but you rob yourselves of interactions that could help you acclimate to the civilian life.

Sixth, practice patience. You need to learn to relax. Take some time, and just let some things slide.

Before we close this chapter of our study, we need to reflect on some ways in which veterans feel that colleges might better serve veterans. I set forth the following concerns that veterans have voiced over the past few years in relation to campus life. I gained these insights from a class that I teach each semester for veterans only.

- The school hasn't provided adequate information on where to go to receive assistance in registering for classes.
- Advisors assume that the veteran knows more about university life than they do. Campuses should recognize that the typical veteran has been out of high school for several years.
- Advisors must urge veterans to start with a lighter load initially (ten to twelve hours) until they are acclimated to university life.
- Advisors must help veterans with their selection of classes, spreading out the more difficult classes over future semesters so that they are not overloaded at first.
- The university needs to plan for the special recognition of veterans on national holidays, such as Memorial Day, Veterans Day, the Fourth of July, etc.

- The veterans need access to mentors who can provide day-to-day advice and recommendations.
- The administration must be cautious in setting forth what the school provides in relation to assisting student veterans. These interactions can often make the veteran feel as if he or she is being used primarily as a tool for the promotion of the school.
- Help prepare the veteran for the transition from the generally peaceful diversity of the military to the presence of racism and bigotry that is often found on some campuses.

Chapter 14

Resiliency

Resilience has been described by Mandy Oaklander as "essentially a set of skills—as opposed to a disposition or personality type—that make it possible for people not only to get through hard times but to thrive during and after them. Just as rubber rebounds after being squeezed or squished, so do resilient people."[48]

Resiliency is defined in the military as the ability to withstand, recover, grow, and adapt under adverse circumstances and to return to a state of readiness for future challenges. Being deployed in the military during a time of war tests the resilience of every man and woman. Veterans carry the weight of an uncontrollable and volatile environment that threatens their actual and perceived well-being as well as their level of resilience. Such often requires resilience adjustment.

The outcome of reduced resiliency, often caused by something as common to post-deployment veterans as poor sleep quality, can be seen in PTSD, suicide, and physical and mental illness resulting from depletion. Such can occur in subtle ways that are not immediately obvious. These factors contribute to substance abuse, domestic strife, and depression, and they also increased the risk of contracting many chronic diseases. The influence of reduced resiliency can have

---

[48] Mandy Oaklander, "Bounce Back," *Time Magazine* 185, no. 20 (2015), 36–42.

long-term effects, and in a sense, this lack fulfills the definition of a chronic illness.[49]

As we see the winding down of the engagement in the Iraq and Afghanistan wars and tens of thousands of soldiers from the US Army, Navy, Marines, Air Force, and National Guard reentering the United States, we must ask, "How can we improve physical and mental resilience of this dedicated group of veterans?"

It is my conviction that we must include in every program of recovery emphasis on single-minded obedience to the call of God through Jesus Christ for the returning Christian veteran. This means that the Christian veteran must include in his or her recovery a reliance on the Word of God through Christ to face the issues of life in conjunction with other approaches to recovery.

As we reflect on what it means to follow Christ in single-minded obedience, let us examine and comment on the following Scriptures:

1. Exodus 14:15—Moses started his journey with excuses (cf. Exodus 3:11–12; 3:13; 4:10–17), and God's Word to him said, "Moses, why are you standing there crying to me; get up and do something." There are times when action is needed, when obedience entails action. Jesus calls for such action. "Take up your bed and walk … Follow me … Go into the world." No excuses from the people are acceptable (cf. Exodus 14:11–12). Get up and do something.
2. 1 John 3:24—The conditions of fellowship with the Holy Spirit and his power within lie in obedience. This is a relational matter. Depend on the Holy Spirit, and allow him to function within. "If by the spirit you put to death the deeds of the body" (Romans 8:14).

---

[49] For those interested in information concerning renewing resiliency, the U.S. Army Medical Command has a program called "Battlemind." "Battlemind" is both the mental orientation developed during a combat zone deployment and a program developed at Walter Reed Army Institute of Research (WRAIR) intended to reduce its impact on personal-deployment issues.

3. Matthew 19:23–26—We try in vain to make things happen, but we are defeated. It is very difficult for a rich man to enter the kingdom of heaven! The disciples were shocked with the demands of discipleship, but success was possible. Many will enter the kingdom of heaven, for God desires all to enter (2 Peter 3:9). "With God all things are possible!" (You may want to especially focus on Matthew 19:24 and the "eye of the needle.")

4. Mark 8:34—Taking up the cross is a voluntary thing, not a handicap or inconvenience that we inherited but something we agree to bear. We are not called to be served but to serve (cf. Mark 10:35–45). The most successful way to recovery is through serving others. This is not a call to self-negation, self-hatred, or timidity. We should not view the self as something without value. It takes courage and resiliency to stand against the world, to identify with the weak and oppressed, and to serve.

5. Luke 9:57–62—Here is a clarion call and definition of discipleship from Luke's account of Jesus' message to some would-be disciples. A reliance on Jesus Christ in assisting one in recovering life involves making Jesus Christ first and foremost in all that one does.

Committing oneself to the lifestyle set forth by Jesus Christ certainly requires courage and perseverance. However, such is essential if we are not to be stymied by fear. Oaklander writes, "So far, researchers have found that facing the things that scare you relaxes the fear circuitry, making that a good first step in building resilience. They have also found that developing an ethical code to guide daily decisions can help. Studies have shown that traits scientists once thought of as nice but unnecessary—like having a strong network of social support – are critical to resilience."[50]

---

[50] Ibid., p. 40.

In relation to developing resilience, here is a list of ten "Expert Tips for Resilience." Since resiliency is the ability of an individual to bounce back from life's adversity and cope with stresses and deal with these stresses in a healthy manner, the below listed tips will be invaluable in developing a stronger resiliency. If you discipline yourself to make these tried and tested tips a regular part of your life, you will be more successful in your future journey.

1) Develop a core set of beliefs that nothing can shake.
2) Try to find meaning in whatever stressful or traumatic thing has happened.
3) Try to maintain a positive outlook.
4) Take cues from someone who is especially resilient.
5) Don't run from things that scare you. Face them.
6) Be quick to reach out for support when things go haywire.
7) Learn new things as often as you can.
8) Find an exercise regimen you'll stick to.
9) Don't beat yourself up or dwell on the past.
10) Recognize what makes you uniquely strong—and own it.[51]

---

[51] Ibid., p. 42.

Chapter 15

Self-Perception

A recent Pew Research study reports that esteem for military personnel still tops the list of various professions. More than three-quarters of US adults (or 78 percent) say that members of the armed services contribute "a lot" to society's well-being. This reflects a slight decline from the 84 percent of four years ago.

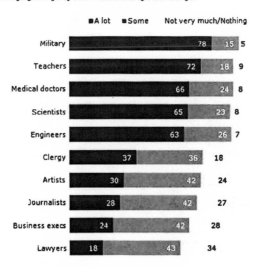

Perceptions of Occupational Groups

% saying each group contributes to society's well-being ...

■A lot ■Some Not very much/Nothing

Group	A lot	Some	Not very much/Nothing
Military	78	15	5
Teachers	72	18	9
Medical doctors	66	24	8
Scientists	65	23	8
Engineers	63	26	7
Clergy	37	36	18
Artists	30	42	24
Journalists	28	42	27
Business execs	24	42	28
Lawyers	18	43	34

Source: Pew Research Center survey March 21-April 8, 2013. Q6a-). Responses of those who did not give an answer are not shown.

PEW RESEARCH CENTER

Perceptions of Occupational Groups

Today, less than 0.5 percent of the US population serves in the military. Compare that with more than 12 percent who served during WWII. Thus, the military has become a rare profession. The fact is that it isn't easy to get into the military, for one has to pass difficult examinations prior to enlisting. Military personnel must also maintain emotional, mental, and psychological well-being in order to sustain the high demand that duty requires.

In addition, there is the sense of honor and pride ingrained within military personnel, something often missing within the civilian populace. The lifestyle is disciplined with early wake-up calls, and it is very mission-focused as well. There is no room for distractions, nonsense, or pettiness. All of this makes for a satisfying and regular state of well-being as well as a sense of accomplishment, duty, and honor.

This results in a promotion of positive and healthy mental health and self-esteem. You know what you do matters. Yet when veterans reintegrate into society, they feel disconnected from all these, and the general public doesn't get this. The public generally has no basic idea of what the veteran sacrifices, especially in times of conflict, and this situation can be frustrating to veterans. Maybe this is why the *vanilla* gratitude offered so many times in public rings somewhat shallow to many veterans.

Some see this cycle continuing for today's veterans. A former veteran named John Prine has written, "That's every war, too. The real trouble of the military, they take your individuality away from you, because you need to be broken down to obey, especially in combat. But then after two or three years, they let you out. It's like prison, because they dump you out into the street-having spent a lot of time brainwashing you—with no help to re-acclimate. So they're lost, and the combat guys are traumatized, and this is what happens."

In relation to self-perception, one of the most meaningful passages in the Bible on human dignity is Psalm 8.

> O LORD, our Lord, how majestic is thy name in all
> the earth!
> Thou whose glory above the heavens is chanted by
> the mouth of babes and infants,
> thou hast founded a bulwark because of thy foes, to
> still the enemy and the avenger.
> When I look at thy heavens, the work of thy fingers,
> the moon and the stars which thou hast established;
> what is man that thou art mindful of him,
> and the son of man that thou dost care for him?
> Yet thou hast made him little less than God,
> and dost crown him with glory and honor.
> Thou hast given him dominion over the works of
> thy hands;
> thou hast put all things under his feet,
> all sheep and oxen, and also the beasts of the fields,
> the birds of the air, and the fish of the sea,
> whatever passes along the paths of the sea.
> O LORD, our Lord, how majestic is thy name in all
> the earth!

The psalmist is amazed at the value the Lord God has placed on humans. In view of this and the second great commandment's admonition to "love your neighbor as yourself" (Leviticus 19:18; Matthew 22:39), how can we not have a healthy self-image? Granted, many veterans have had their self-esteem badly damaged and crippled because of events and situations they may have been involved in during war. Such things and situations may have caused many to believe they had no value and did not deserve to feel good about themselves. To help combat such feelings, we need to reflect on the following descriptions applied to humanity:[52] In each of the following descriptions, read the scriptures assigned to each section prior to reading the materials following.

We are Regarded – John 15:5; Ephesians 1:4; Galatians 4:7; Hebrews 2:11.

"What is man that thou art mindful of him, and the son of man that thou dost care for him? Yet thou hast made him little less that God, and dost crown him with glory and honor?" (Psalm 8:4–5). The psalmist sets forth the very fact that we are regarded by God. We have sinned and fallen short of God's intent, and we have separated ourselves from God. However, he is not satisfied to leave us that way. He reverses the process and seeks to restore each individual to the original intent of his creation. We are made in his image. Therefore, we are to be regarded. This ought to make an enormous difference in our relationships with others.

In Ephesians, Paul dares to suggest that in the midst of us creating disunity between what we think of ourselves and what others think of us, God has created unity out of disunity, order out of disorder, harmony out of disharmony, and peace out of inner strife. Alongside our feelings of being disregarded, God has brought us into being regarded and valued. We must recognize that we are made to be in him and regarded.

We are important - Matthew 5:13-14; John 1:12.

In a world where importance is measured by those who reach worldly heights and follow ambition, Jesus points out that we are to be as essential to life as salt and light. As believers, we bring out the flavor of the world as God meant for it, and we are sources of enlightenment, an enlightenment that sees life as a prize rather than a burden. What more does the world today need than these things?

---

[52] Adsit, *The Combat Trauma Healing Manual* (Newport News, VA: Military Ministry Press, 2008), 97-108.

What does Jesus mean when he says to his followers, "You are the salt and light of the world?" He means that we will illuminate dishonest practices, promote justice in the social and political arena, and fight against prejudice, greed, and selfishness. And these important people (disciples) of Christ are those who reflect his light to the world. Christians are truly the hope of the world.

We are forgiven - Romans 5:1; 8:1; Hebrews 10:17.

These are comforting Scriptures. "Therefore, since we are justified by faith, we have peace with God through our Lord Jesus Christ ... There is therefore now no condemnation for those who are in Christ Jesus ... I will remember their sins and their misdeeds no more." We will always fail (cf. Romans 3:10, 23), and this will always be true. We cannot atone for our sins, for only God can do this. Our part is to do nothing more than throw ourselves on his grace and accept with full confidence what only he is prepared to give. This does not mean that we become righteous, for sin will always be there, but it does mean that God see us as "righteous in Christ."

This does not mean, however, that we can continue in sin so that grace may abound (cf. Romans 6:1). It means that Christ has come to us as a lasting possession and the he brings with him the power to make our will victorious. This is what Romans 8:1–17 is all about.

We are valued - Jeremiah 31:2; Romans 8:29–30; 1 Corinthians 6:19–20).

In the Jeremiah passage, we see God's people in Babylonian captivity, broken. They have lost their temple, homeland, and way of life because of their past sinful lifestyles. Yet in the midst of all this fragmentation in life, God never gave up on his people. In the same manner, he will never give up on us, for we are valued. He will, as indicated in Romans 8:29–30, work all things out in our lives so that he will always be working for our highest good. And he will also dwell within us, for we are the temple of God, the dwelling place of God's Holy Spirit.

So, even when we might be in the darkness and pain because of negative situations in our lives, God will always be present with us with a light of hope and recovery. We can be very sure of God and cling to him in all circumstances. In the words of Paul, "May the God of hope fill you with all joy and peace in believing, so that by the power of the Holy Spirit you may abound in hope" (Romans 15:13).

Chapter 16

Now What? Getting Back to Normalcy

Now that we have gone through many of the possible situations that we may have to face in our post-deployment life, what can we expect? This final chapter will be concerned primarily with the family life of a returning veteran since this aspect of life is the very foundation of any quality of life that we may hope to develop.

How long will it be before we start walking down the road to what may be described as normalcy? All of the exciting and heartwarming airport welcomes, parades, flag-waving, and other celebrations are behind us. Returning home from deployment can be a time of incredible happiness, but as things wind down, are we expected to return to normalcy?

We often hear that you cannot go back home, meaning that things will never be the same as they were when you left. Therefore, we must recognize the need to face adjustment following a return home. Time changes things, both for the good and sometimes the not so good. What will happen, however, is that you will develop a new normal. The reality is that physical, spiritual, and emotional health and welfare are all connected. Taking care of these aspects will increase the likelihood of recovering normalcy. With this in mind, we need to be keenly aware of some important principles to develop and live by as we transition to this new normal. While these principles will not be a one-size-fits-all solution, they will assist us as we get to know and trust the family and community again and return to normalcy.

Communication

Coupled with listening and consideration for the feelings of others, communication is a key element in developing this new normalcy. According to a recent *Wall Street Journal* survey in relation to marriage relationships, 40 percent of the respondents stated that lack of time together was a greater problem for them than a lack of money (Graham and Crossan, 1996). It is through open and honest communication that you and your partner feel that individual needs are understood and respected and that these are priorities in your life. Through listening, you also have opportunity to identify and work through conflicts that are a very real part of every marriage.

Family Communication Checklist

Examine the following statements listed below and respond to them. Answer True or False for each statement. If you wish, check your impressions against those in your family, having the family member take the same true/false questions. After writing the responses to the questions on a sheet of paper, evaluate your family's responses and let your family evaluate you.

1. I clearly say what I mean. **True False**
2. I am an attentive and sympathetic listener. **True False**
3. When I do not understand, I ask questions. **True False**
4. I let other people finish talking before I speak. **True False**
5. I am straightforward and forthright in expressing my thoughts and feelings. **True False**
6. I rarely use sarcasm and insults. **True False**

7. I willingly listen to the ideas and feelings of others. **True False**

8. When stating an opinion, I use phrases like "I think" and "It seems to me." **True False**

9. I seldom get angry or hostile when someone disagrees with me. **True False**

10. I am sensitive to nonverbal signals like tone of voice and body language. **True False**

The more trues you have, the more skillful you are as a communicator. What can you learn from this? Are there aspects of communication that you need to work on?

Family Activities

There is a prevalent tendency to spend time connecting with former wartime buddies because no one understands a veteran's situation better than those who have been there. A major problem faced by many spouses is the feeling that his or her veteran spouse often shares feelings and seeks comfort from war buddies more often than from the family. This strong bond between veterans, promoted by shared experiences is necessary from time to time, but do not neglect the very people who love you the most and have your best interests at heart—your family.

You cannot disconnect and withdraw from family, no matter how much such isolation may seem like a good thing. Working toward developing family relationships and interaction is a great stress reliever and a most effective way to achieve calmness. Again, time with family is so important, for the family will typically listen without judging and criticizing. This can be a source of strength and comfort. And what better place is there to create your own safe place to calm any trouble than with your family?

Patience

Be patient. The prophet Habakkuk says, "For still the vision awaits its time; it hastens to the end—it will not lie. If it seems slow, wait for it; it will surely come, it will not delay" (Habakkuk 2:3). As a veteran, you have experienced a lot in your deployment. The transition out of the mental and emotional war zone that you may still experience won't happen overnight. You have been away from your loved ones and a former way of life, and the process of getting back to normal can take several months. The family time you may have missed cannot be regained overnight, especially when you have children. In our fast-track and hurry-up society, we find it so difficult to delay gratification. Yet anything worth achieving is going to have obstacles along the way. Take things day by day, and you will discover that God's timing is perfect.

Partnership with God

Make God a partner. Augustine is credited with saying about God, "You have created us for yourself and our hearts are restless until they rest in you." The good news on recovery from whatever *shalom*-threatening situation we face is that we have been given the privilege of partnership with God. We have previously seen that God values us above all else that he has created. "What is man that thou art mindful; of him, and the son of man that thou dost care for him? Yet thou hast made him little less than God and dost crown him with glory and honor" (Psalm 8:4–5).

One of the great songs of faith is titled, "No, Never Alone." This means that God is never just "up there" and that I am just "down here." It means that God is always with me. With his presence, we can conquer any situation, and we need never despair. As Paul says, nothing "in all creation, will be able to separate us from the love of God in Christ Jesus our Lord" (Romans 8:39). If we are not in a relationship with God, we are far less than what we are capable of being. As stated before, religious faith is among the most important factors that influence the reentry process. This finding is consistent with other studies of the general population and suggests religious belief is correlated with a number of positive outcomes, including better physical and emotional health as well as happier and more satisfying personal relationships.[53] Jesus puts it in this way: "Apart from me [God] you can do nothing" (John 15:5). We must, therefore, partner with God and make him a very real part of our daily lives. To do otherwise would be foolish.

Self-Care

Take care of yourself. As health care professionals emphasize, your body and mind need support and care. Maintaining a fit, nourished, and healthy body is essential for proper functioning in life. It is common for veterans to experience insomnia, fatigue, irritably, and angry outbursts. It is also common for veterans to be drawn to activities and behaviors that give one an adrenaline rush. Thus, veterans seek energy drinks, coffee, stimulant drugs, and other things that may promote addiction in their efforts to manage stress. A better route may involve finding time to rest, limiting the use of alcohol, finding ways to relax, seeking proper exercise, and maintaining a balanced and nutritious diet.

---

[53] http>//.pewsocial trends.org/2011/12/08/the-difficult-transition-from-military-to-civilian-life.

Epilogue

I close this book after a long but very informative journey on my part. My research and writing on this subject matter have been ongoing for more than three years now, not counting my forty-plus years in the ministry, growing and developing my faith in God as well as my limited knowledge of his Word and how it applies to each of our lives. I have also taught several classes on the university campus, classes for veterans only. Much of the material I presented in these classes was used in this book.

My greatest hope is that the ideas spelled out in this book will help our veterans, their spouses, families, and friends come to positions in life where they truly realize what God desires them to gain—a peace (*shalom*) that passes all understanding. If this book has in some way been useful to you reaching this desired goal, then the time and effort will have been well worth my endeavor, and I will continue to present the material in both book form and future university classes designed for our brave men and women, our veterans.

Appendix: The Christian and War

What the Bible Says About Christian Soldiers

Over the years I have engaged from time to time in a serious study concerning what Scripture says about the Christian's relation to war. This is a subject that has deeply divided the church since its beginning in the first century of our era. This is a very complex question. I want you to know that I am not pro-war, but I'm not a conscientious objector either. So I present this material from the background of a former Marine and one who is heavily involved with post-deployed veterans on this Lipscomb University campus, as a faculty member in the College of Bible and Ministry, and as chaplain to the student veterans.

The quest for peace has always been one of our goals as Christians, yet this quest is always overshadowed by war and threat of war. War distorts lives and threatens the very survival of humanity. Nations fear expansionist ambitions of neighboring nations. We stockpile weapons. Terrorists abound. So what does the Bible have to say about the Christian and war?

The Bible and war are two very complex subjects. The question of war and Christian participation in war has been around since the early days of the beginnings of humanity. With this fact in mind, we cannot do justice to the question of the Christian and war without speaking of the Hebrew Scriptures, the New Testament, and the Ante-Nicene Fathers. This in itself would require a full semester to examine, far more time than we have in this conference. Thankfully, my task is not to do this but to limit my remarks to what the Bible says about Christian soldiers, thus examining the New Testament teachings and insinuations on this subject. Of course, this will involve a word or two from time to time from both the Old Testament and the Ante-Nicene Fathers.

Obviously God commanded in the Law, "You shall not kill," a command repeated by Jesus in the Sermon on the Mount. But does this settle the issue? What about the law, "Whoever sheds man's blood, by man shall his blood be shed, for in the image of God he made man" (Genesis 9:6)? Apparently, this gives men acting collectively (the state) the right to administer capital punishment and to *designate individuals* to carry this out!

Equally obvious, God instructed his people to raise armies and to kill the enemy. So does he prohibit believers from engaging in war under any circumstances? What about God's use of nations to carry out justice and judgment, even against his own people? At this time, I don't think we want to get into the debate about Israel as a theocracy or that the Old Testament ethical system was supposedly not as high as the New Testament system or that God has somehow changed his ethics in the New Testament era. This must be reserved for another time.

Old Testament believers lived under an ethical system that condemned revenge, limited self-defense, and encouraged loving fellow Jews and foreigners, as is the ethical system for New Testament believers. For example, what the priest and Levite did in Jesus' Samaritan parable was contrary to the Mosaic law (cf. Luke 10:30–37). Paul quotes from the Old Testament in Romans 12:19–21 about the importance of peace toward enemies. Thus, the Old Testament taught a personal ethic of nonretaliation and nonviolence along with the need for kindness to all in need. Yet the Old Testament does not see this as inconsistent in relation to its emphasis on the call for personal self-defense and just wars in defense of the nation.

Well, what about the New Testament? We recall the narrative of John the Baptizer telling soldiers not to misuse their power, yet he says nothing about leaving the military (cf. Luke 3:10–14). And in the Sermon on the Mount, Jesus taught us to love the neighbor, turn the other cheek, give the cloak, etc. There is indisputable New Testament evidence that Jesus encountered believers who were in the Roman Army—a centurion who sent the Jewish elders to ask Jesus to heal his servant who was about to die (cf. Matthew 8:5–13; Luke 7:1–10), about whom Jesus said, "I have not found such faith in all Israel." Yet Jesus never stated that military service on the part of these believers is contrary to God's will in these situations.

This same principle is true in relation to the centurion at the foot of the cross exclaiming of Jesus, "Surely he was [the, a] son of God" (Matthew 27:54); to Cornelius, a centurion responding to the gospel as preached by Peter (cf. Acts 10); or when Paul speaks of his imprisonment in the palace jail resulting in the conversion of some within the palace guard (cf. Philippians 1:13).

In relation to the Sermon on the Mount, it must be remembered that these words were personal admonitions addressed to individuals, not the state. This sermon is a call to *personal* ethics, not national ethics. The individual believer must accept abuse and even death rather than deny Christ yet surely must defend others and a nation against injustice. We should not avenge ourselves but are to live peaceably. Paul put it this manner: "If possible live at peace" (Romans 12:17–21). However, if God gives the leaders of the state, ministers ordained by him, the right to resist evil through war, police forces, etc., cannot the Christian support and join in the promotion of such justice?

Does the New Testament teach that Christians should passively bear verbal and physical abuse against themselves as well as others? Would doing so not allow continuing injustice and harm, thus setting aside the command to love (and all that *love* entails) one who is in a dangerous situation? We may forgo resistance toward us individually, but if turning the other cheek leads to further abuse, I believe it is *no longer possible* (recalling Paul's word of Romans 12) to live at peace if we do not stop the abuse. Did Jesus "turn the other cheek" when he was struck by the officer and replied, "Why do you strike me?" (John 18:23). Or when he drove out the money changers in the temple (cf. John 25)? And if one can do this as an individual, can't one also do this to promote the welfare of a nation?

While on trial for his life, Paul responded to one of the authorities, who ordered him to be struck for blasphemy, "God shall smite you, you whitened wall" (Acts 23:3). Paul's following apology was not that he didn't have the right to challenge his mistreatment, for this was according to the Law, but an apology for the sharpness with which he addressed the high priest.

It is obvious from the Ante-Nicene writings that Christians did serve in the Roman Army in the early days of the church. Yes, pacifism was prevalent in the early church; however, this was not the only or even dominant view of this time period. The fact that the Ante-Nicene writings are concerned with this subject matter indicates that believers were serving in the military!

I believe that the evidence points out that a Christian may resist injustice in any society and can serve in the military, police force, etc. I further believe that it must be a just war or just cause that leads to such activity on the part of the believer. I do not believe the Christian can fight in an unjust war, with the burden of proof of the righteousness of such resistance being on the individual Christian more than the state. However, if I dissent and choose not to engage in war, I must be willing to face the consequences of such dissent.

I recognize the right of those who refuse to participate in war, because they believe such participation would violate their understanding of Jesus' pacifism. This does not mean they cannot serve their nation, however, for we have in the United States opportunities to serve, such as the Peace Corps, Vista, corpsmen, etc. Many of these pacifists turn the other cheek and place their lives in jeopardy, as they refuse to bear arms. However, does one have the right to place other lives in jeopardy because he or she refuses to strike down evil?

We must also address the question, "Is war a moral evil?" I know of no one, General of the Army, veterans of wars, and present-day civil forces, who delight in war. It is a social evil and is of the Devil (cf. James 4:1–2). However, it is not totally evil, or God would not have commanded it to be initiated by his own people. In addition, history bears it out that some good has resulted from wars in spite of the fact that most wars are both unnecessary and wrongfully motivated. I hear that war brings death instead of life. In just one example, did the call to war by the Allied Forces in WWII save thousands of Jews and others from extermination in Nazi Germany?

Scripture never calls war a moral evil as such. Evil lies behind hell, but it is morally necessary just as jails, criminal courts, and wars are. If war was morally evil, would we read of Michael and his angels at war with the Devil and his angels or the military figures and symbols in Scripture? Would Miriam be characterizing God as promoting evil when she said, "The Lord is a man of war, the Lord is his name" (Exodus 15:3)?

Is it right for civil rulers to use coercive force? Can the state serve as a police force in order to save lives and promote peace when it fights against mobs destroying a city? If so, then is it right for Christians to be a part of that force for good? Or has God designated one section of the society to do something as a matter of necessity and duty that the conscientious believer is forbidden to do, for some think it involves sin?

Here we must spend a moment discussing violence. This is a call for the understanding of the word violence and what such entails. We hear a lot about the issues of violence and nonviolence. Violence is often defined as "inflicting suffering on others, hurting or killing or forcefully taking advantage of others." Yet the Old and New Testaments speak of vengeance, retribution, and punishment, all of which can and often do involve violence. Paul, like Jesus, tells Christians to return good for evil, exhibit loving service to neighbors and enemies. Paul further teaches that personal vengeance is off-limits (cf. Romans 12:19), and that God is the one to execute vengeance. At times God will use governments to carry out his justice, and this often entails force and violence. So if Christians find themselves in positions of governing authority, do they not then become servants of God's justice rather than being personal vengeance-takers or promoters of personal violence?

The key word in all the discussions on the right of believers to bear arms is *peacemaking*. Again, Paul writes, "If it be *possible* as far as it depends on you, live at peace with everyone" (Romans 12:18 NIV). Peace was at the very heart of conquering the Promised Land. The Mosaic law states, "When you draw near to a city to fight against it, offer terms of peace to it. And if its answer to you is peace and it opens to you, then all the people who are found in it shall do forced labor for you and shall serve you. But if it makes no peace with you, but makes war against you, then you shall besiege it; and when the Lord your God gives it into your hands you shall put all its males to the sword" (Deuteronomy 20:10–13).

In conclusion, what is my position in regards to the state and war? I do not have the competence to give omniscient guidance. We search in vain for any adequate, timeless statement of a *just war*. There are many doctrines of the just war, which are the result of sincere spiritual insights and common sense. We differ on these. However, one thing we do agree on, and that is we cannot as Christians worship the state, any country, or any leader other than our Lord God. We cannot violate our conscience. Neither can we judge another whose position concerning resisting evil differs from ours. We also have a responsibility to exercise the task of holding accountable those who commit unjust aggression against our neighbor while working for the restraint of personal vengeance. In addition, we can and must pray for our rulers and our nation, and we must seek peace always as the first priority.

Blessed are the peacemakers. Who are the peacemakers? Those who serve in the Peace Corps, run schools, produce crops, serve in medical fields, stay at home, and minister to churches? Is it possible that they could also be those who fight in military campaigns to bring justice and challenge corrupt civil orders? I choose to say that all of these are peacemakers.[54]

---

[54] This is a message that I (Tom Seals) delivered during the "Hazilip-Series Summer Celebration" at Lipscomb University, Nashville, TN, July 2, 2015.

CPSIA information can be obtained
at www.ICGtesting.com
Printed in the USA
FFOW02n0111120816
26750FF